Life
Without
A Centre

LIFE
WITHOUT
A CENTRE

✳

Awakening from
the Dream of Separation

JEFF FOSTER

NON-DUALITY PRESS

For my family

NON-DUALITY PRESS
6 Folkestone Road Salisbury SP2 8JP United Kingdom
www.non-dualitybooks.com

Copyright © Jeff Foster 2006
First printing December 2006

Cover concept and photography: Sally Bongers and Paul Elliot
Layout: John Gustard

For more information visit:
www.geocities.com/thisispresence/

Isbn: 0-9553999-0-4
Isbn complete: 978-0-9553999-0-9

"And what then is action without a centre, what then is life without a centre? ... Having a centre is the very essence of sorrow. The centre creates the tomorrow..."

J. Krishnamurti

"The Life I am trying to grasp is the me that is trying to grasp it."

R. D. Laing, *The Bird of Paradise*

Contents

Introduction

"All the world's a stage,
and all the men and women merely players..."
- Shakespeare

This is all there is, although in a thousand different ways we spend our lives searching for something more.

And what is *this?*

Present sights, present sounds, present smells, present thoughts. Present memories of the past, present ideas of what the future may hold. Present ideas of "wanting an end to problems" or "wanting spiritual enlightenment" or "wanting to awaken". Present ideas of "myself" or "me" or "I" or "my difficult life and all its problems". Present breathing, present beating of the heart, present gas bills piled up on the kitchen table, present miaowing of the cat, present screaming of children out in the street, present pain in the chest, present longing for something "more than this", present feeling of frustration at "not getting it", present desire to be free from it all.

Watch a child at play. For them, it seems, this life is a great game, a giant playground where everything fascinates, and there seems to be little desire to escape from life and all its problems, to move into some higher or more "spiritual" dimension. As adults, however, we seem to spend a lot of time trying to escape from the play of life and all the suffering that being "a person in the world" inevitably entails. Drink, drugs, sex, money and meditation are common methods of escape.

And, of course, there is much traditional and contemporary spirituality which is more than happy to cater to the same desire. However, in catering to this desire, the idea that there is, in fact, an individual who could escape from suffering in the first place, or indeed do anything at all, is inevitably reinforced.

In this book, the possibility is suggested that there is only ever the present appearance of life, with no individual at its core who could ever escape even if they wanted to. Indeed, the individual is merely another appearance in the play, not something that needs to be accepted or rejected, transcended or denied, but something that simply appears, along with all the other sights, sounds, smells, thoughts and feelings.

This message is so simple, so obvious. The individual (the seeker, the sufferer, the candlestick maker) simply *appears* as another part of the play of life. And with it may come the desire to escape from life, but that too is merely another appearance, another part of the narrative.

And all of this is absolutely fine; none of it needs to be accepted or rejected, transcended or denied. Suffering is fine, seeking some sort of spiritual enlightenment or liberation is fine, precisely because there is nobody there that any of this happens for, or to, in the first place. "A person at the centre of it all" is just another appearance, another belief, another part of the story.

But don't misunderstand me, I'm not saying we should get rid of our beliefs. Beliefs are fine, and the need for the destruction or transcendence of beliefs would just be another belief anyway. And so, this book will not offer the individual – that is, "you"– any new beliefs, nor will it attempt to destroy any present ones. *Nothing* ever needs to be denied or rejected for liberation to be, because in this moment, as life plays out, there is always *already* liberation, and anything we do to achieve liberation is simply misguided, but nonetheless perfectly acceptable.

Already nobody is running this show, already nobody is suffering and already nobody longs to be free. There is simply the present appearance of it all. Simply *this*, and nothing more. It's so simple, so obvious.

Beyond belief or lack of it, beyond anything that words could ever state, beyond all beyonds, there is always this, now and forever.

*

And not even the recognition or intellectual understanding of any of the above is necessary for liberation, as so often we are told. None of these words need to be understood; there is nothing to "get", nothing to transcend, nothing to be achieved. Lack of understanding, lack of "getting it", lack of achievement: these are yet more present appearances in the play of life, no worse nor better than their opposites.

And all opposites unravel in *this*.

About This Book

This book was written over a two year period, as the desperate search for an escape from life began to be seen through. The seeing-through was sometimes dramatic, sometimes subtle, and always hard to talk about without sounding like a complete self-contradiction.

However, this book emerged somehow, and eventually found its way into those hands either side of these pages.

But before we go any further, here are some disclaimers:

• In this book, no methods are laid out, no "path to self-realization" is set forth. There is no seven-step plan to happiness, no "20 Days To A More Enlightened You!". If things were that easy, why would we all still be searching?

• There is no logical progression in this book. Nothing follows on from anything else, and the text is riddled with paradoxes and contradictions. However, the writing consistently points back to the simplest but most profound of messages: *This is all there is*. This constant reminding of the utterly obvious will not be of any help to "you", the individual, but as the message begins to "permeate" (for want of a better word), and as the apparent existence of the separate individual is seen through, or not, an ease and an equanimity may be revealed...

• This book will not help you. But perhaps, in spite of this book, there will be a seeing through of the need to be helped. Perhaps there will be a seeing through of the search for spiritual enlightenment, the search for Nirvana, the search for peace, the search for liberation and awakening. Or perhaps there won't be any seeing through of the search, and that is fine too. Nothing is required of you.

• This book is not a *prescription* for an individual who seeks answers, but a *description*, for nobody, of what is always already the case. But ultimately, of course, it's not about the words at all. Because this – look! listen! – *is* it. There is nothing more. There never was. The search was always in vain, the search always implied that this wasn't enough. But this is all there is! And so really, this book is not necessary. Treat it like a novel – it's just a bit of fun. Just a story, like any other. Just a collection of black marks on white pages. Liberation is as much "in" the black marks as it is "in" the white spaces.

• There is no "spiritual" content to this message (which, paradoxically, may make it perhaps the most "spiritual" message of all!). What is being said is utterly simple, utterly obvious, utterly ordinary. It's as simple as doing the dishes, as obvious as the sound of the rain falling on the roof, as ordinary as going to the toilet. It's so simple, obvious and ordinary, in fact, that it's nearly always overlooked...

• Read this book slowly. Let it penetrate, percolate, permeate. If you find yourself rushing through it, ask yourself why. What do you want from it? What are you trying to achieve? What are you waiting for? Are you waiting for something to "click"? Are you waiting for enlightenment to descend upon you in a flash of lightning? Are you waiting to "understand"? Do you feel that you "nearly understand" (and isn't that the same as waiting to understand)? Virtually every sentence in this book is pointing at the same thing. If you don't "get it" from the first page of the book, you won't "get it" at all. Because really there's nothing to "get". As long as there is the belief that there is "something to get", there will appear to be something to get. Get it?

*

The three sections of this book represent three aspects of liberation. Part One reflects the utter simplicity and obviousness of liberation: it is *this, here, now* – no attainment necessary! Part Two contains expressions of the undeniable sense of freedom and release that may (or may not) arise as the existence of the apparent individual is seen through. Part Three reflects the way in which liberation seemingly "permeates" the apparent life story of the individual. As seeking subsides, certain aspects of life are seen in new ways. It is not a rejection of the life story, but a seeing through of its apparent solidity. Additionally, there are two sections of dialogues about the search for liberation, enlightenment, happiness, God, Nirvana, a bigger bank balance.

And now, on with the show.

PART ONE

Liberation: Here and Now

*"I have never wanted to live seriously. I've been able
to put on a show – to know pathos, and anguish,
and joy. But never, never have I known seriousness.
My whole life has been just a game: sometimes long and
tedious, sometimes in bad taste – but a game."*

– Jean-Paul Sartre

Hooked on Enlightenment

I first appeared on the stage of life some 26 years ago, playing the role of a shy and introverted child. Some years later, I acted the part of a painfully self-conscious teenager. Later still, a horribly depressed and self-conscious twenty-something moped around the stage. Then, at the age of 23, after a relatively serious bout of depression followed by a nasty illness (very well acted, I must say) I caught the spiritual bug. I wanted spiritual enlightenment, liberation, release from all my suffering, an escape from the human condition! I wanted to transcend the "ego", to put an end to "me and my problems", to lose my "self", to merge with God and leave my miserable human life behind!

I ploughed through hundreds of religious/spiritual books by dozens of wise men, gurus, teachers and heavily bearded philosophers. And I read and I read, and I meditated and ate vegetarian food and listened to poor quality mp3's of happy Indian people telling me what a wonderful thing it was to have a "silent mind", and yet the yearning to be free still burned more fiercely than ever. How could I attain this state of utter stillness and peacefulness that these so-called "enlightened" people had apparently stumbled across? I certainly had moments of peace, stillness and clarity, but how could I make this permanent? How could I dwell in Heaven all the time? How could I escape my "ordinary life" once and for all? How could I be free from myself and all my so-called "psychological baggage"?

I was hooked on enlightenment.

*

Fast forward to today, and the search is over, or more accurately, it has been seen through. Or, more accurately, it IS being seen through, now, now and now.

There is, of course, no such thing as enlightenment, there is no "ultimate" state, no way to meditate one's way to Nirvana, no way to "get rid" of the ego. *These are just more desires of the ego, more ways to maintain the separate self-sense, the sense of "I".*

The search implies that there is something more to life than what is presently the case. But the search is in vain, for there is only ever *this*. Only this! The feeling of the book between the hands. The beating of the heart. The morning traffic rumbling outside. The cat begging for food. Why do we search for liberation when it is always here?

*

So, after years of searching and never finding, the futility of it all has been (is being) seen through. This ordinary life is already what we are looking for, and already, in this moment, we have everything we need. This seems so damn difficult to see when we are on the spiritual path; indeed, any path to freedom implies by its very existence that freedom is *not* here, that liberation is *not* this, that this moment is *not* enough.

It seems that we want and need a future in which there is some happiness better than the present happiness. The idea that this is all there is, that this moment is life's only meaning, that this moment is all we have or ever will have, is very challenging to a mind locked into the idea of a future salvation. *"This? This can't be it!"*, we cry.

But this is it! This is liberation, enlightenment, God (call it what you will!). And if there is seeking in this moment, then do not despair: that too is liberation, enlightenment, God. Liberation includes anything and everything.

This cannot be understood on an intellectual level, or for that matter, on any level at all. The drive to "understand" this would just be more seeking. *"When I understand this, all seeking will fall away and I'll be enlightened"*, we say to ourselves. But the current lack of understanding is yet another present appearance, and that too is liberation, enlightenment, God.

When the desire to escape from the present is seen through, there is a great ease, a great "okayness" about everything, no matter what happens. This is not something that can be achieved, but something that already is. Already, there is this ease, but perhaps it is "obscured" by our incessant seeking for something more. Of course, it can never really be obscured. It is what we are. It is *this*. It is *now*.

This will never leave us. *This* will always be *this*. *This* is home.

*

And so these days, there is just the living of a very ordinary life, with no desire to reach some higher plane of existence, find my "True Self", or become one with God.

And it's so obvious to me now: *This ordinary life is all there is, or ever was.* There was never anything to find in the first place, because nothing had ever been lost.

In hindsight, doesn't it all seem so silly?

The End of the Search

This is it. This is the end of the spiritual search. Freedom and happiness and enlightenment are to be found nowhere else but here: right in front of us.

The low hum of the computer fan, a tingling feeling in the left foot, the tweet-tweet of the little birdies in the garden, hopping from branch to branch....

Why are we never satisfied with *this*? Why is this moment never enough?

Perhaps it is because at some point in our lives we picked up the belief that there exists something More Than This; some sort of state in which our True Nature™ is revealed to us in all its glory, in which all thoughts dissolve, in which the ego burns up and vanishes for all time, leaving no trace. Some state, in other words, that is very different from this present state.

But what reality does any of that have? Right now, there is only the sound of the little robin jumping about in the tree over there, the beating of the heart, the steam rising from a freshly brewed cup of tea, the morning breeze gently caressing my cheek...

And then the thought "There must be more than this! I'm not there now, but soon, one day, maybe, maybe even in a few minutes, I'll reach that state that I've read so much about! That state of no-state, that freedom, that release!"

But the thought "There must be more to life than this" arises now. It is a present thought, as all thoughts are. *All thoughts are present thoughts. All sounds are present sounds, all sights are present sights.* The present can never be escaped: thought is just the *illusion* of past and future.

And if there is only ever the present, then this state of enlightenment, of liberation, or whatever you want to call it, must be achieved in the present. Which is to say, *it cannot be achieved at all.* Because an achievement implies time, implies a self. Someone to achieve, and a time when it will be achieved.

Hopeless, hopeless, hopeless!

There is only ever now. There is only ever this. The search for something other than this is a denial of the undeniable *thisness* of this, the undeniable presence of being. The search for enlightenment is a denial of the enlightenment that *always already* is. The search for oneness is a denial of ... oh, you get the idea.

And the paradox goes even deeper. Because even the search for oneness, for liberation, for release, for freedom ... even the search is simply an expression of oneness, liberation, release, freedom.

It cannot be found, it cannot be escaped, it cannot be avoided.

*

And so, after a lifetime of searching, the utterly obvious reveals itself. And the utterly obvious is always right in front of us.

AND THIS IS IT!

This is oneness! This is liberation! It cannot be lost, it cannot be found. It cannot be avoided, it cannot be ignored. Avoid it, and it is simply oneness avoiding oneness. Ignore it, and oneness is ignoring oneness. Try to find it, and it is oneness trying to find oneness.

So what to do?

Is there still seeking?

That's fine.

Is there still pain?

That's fine too.

Is there suffering, hope, despair?

That's all fine. Nothing else is needed. Nothing more, nothing less.

The end of the search is a radical, radical acceptance of what is. And this acceptance, this seeing through, is not done by you. It is not a doing. It is not an achievement. Not something to be strived for.

*

So, there may be seeing through, or there may not. There may be absorption in the search, or there may be a sense of ease, a feeling of release. It's all fine, it's all wonderful, it's all part of the play.

There may be a little robin hopping from branch to branch, and it may be seen (or not) that there is *only* the robin, there is *only* the hop-hop-hopping, there is *only* the "tweet-tweet". All this is oneness. Without beginning or end. Without purpose or goal or meaning.

The little robin doesn't give two hoots (tweets?) about finding itself, or reaching a state of liberation. For it, just the hopping, just the search for the next worm is enough, it seems. Perhaps that's why we're so drawn to nature. Animals seem to be so free of the burden of individuality, of selfhood, of the search for something more meaningful than what is already the case.

But the great liberation is already here, for all of us. This – what is already clearly given in this moment – is all the meaning there is. This – sitting on the toilet, or eating lunch, or buying bread and milk from the local shop – is all the purpose there is.

It is the very search for purpose that creates purposelessness, and it is the search for meaning that creates meaninglessness.

*

There is nothing more than this. Fall in love with it... or not. You know, it doesn't really matter either way. There is nothing to be gained by seeing this. This is not an achievement, it is not the result of a long struggle, it is nothing to do with intelligence or skill or knowledge. It is nothing to do with cause or effect, with effort or persistence or anything else.

Freedom and enlightenment are to be found nowhere else but here. Which is to say, they cannot be "found" at all.

Liberation Is...

Liberation is…

Liberation is…

Liberation is…

Liberation is…

Liberation is…

Liberation is…

Liberation is…

Liberation is…

Liberation is…

The Divine Paradox

I am simply not here.

What you see when you look this way is a bag of flesh and bone that is seen to act in certain, sometimes predictable, ways and emits certain, sometimes predictable, sounds (and smells!). You see all this, and you know it as "Jeff". That is your me. That is me, to you.

But is there a "me" over here to which you are referring? Is there a "Jeff" in here that you are somehow recognising and putting a name to?

*

Over here, there is open space, filled with sights and sounds and smells and thoughts and feelings. But – and here's the great discovery – there is simply no "me" to be found at the centre of it all, no "me" in charge of things. "Me" or "I" or "myself" is just *another* part of the scenery, along with all the other present sights and sounds and smells. "Me" is a present appearance like everything else: the humming of traffic, the tweeting of the birds, the beating of the heart. Just another object of experience.

This is all there is: *Present sights and sounds and smells, present life playing out, but no "me" at the centre of it all; no "me" in control.*

*

So when you look over here at this bag of flesh and bone and its associated behaviours, and when you address it as "Jeff", there is a response here, because there is the deeply engrained knowledge that this sort of thing is appropriate – to respond to the name that the bag of flesh and bone and its associated behaviour has been given. Not to respond would be socially unacceptable, and this bag of flesh and bone may be cast into the loony bin, or at least heavily medicated.

And yet, one can't help wondering that perhaps it is dishonest to answer to a name, to identify who I am with who the world says I am. Because I certainly do not experience myself as a person, as an individual, as a thing-in-the-world. No: if "I" am anything, I am this open space, in which the whole world appears, and indeed "I" am not separate from this world which appears. If I am anything, I am what is happening, right here, right now, in this moment. If I am anything, I am *this, this and this.*

"Jeff" does not even begin to capture it. "Jeff" is a relic from the past, part of a narrative that everybody seems to spin for themselves and by themselves. Indeed, there seem to be as many Jeffs as there are people who apparently know him.

This is not to deny that there is an idea here of a "Jeff" floating about in awareness, as thought. But that is all there is, over here. There is no Jeff having thoughts of "Jeff" – that's the illusion. There is only the thought of "Jeff" here, only the narrative floating through.

And it happens for nobody, it arises in this open space, it arises now. And there is simply no "Jeff" outside of that. Which is to say, there is no "Jeff" at all. I simply do not exist. "I" am simply not here.

No self, no problem, as an old Zen monk once said.

*

And yet, and yet... to all intents and purposes, I *do* exist. In the eyes of the world, anyway, there most definitely is a Jeff – he has a birth certificate and a National Insurance number and everything! To function in the world, a basic assumption seems to be necessary: that there is an individual here, a person. But it is an assumption, an idea, nothing more, and it has no deeper reality.

And with that, the entire world self-liberates, because there is simply no "me" to expect anything of it, to make demands of it, to claim to know how any of it works. Freed from the stranglehold of thought, freed from the burden of "me and all my problems", there is a great ease which permeates everything. Freed from goals and meanings, every moment is a goal in itself, everything is intrinsically meaningful, because every moment is all there is, or ever was. Freed from self-consciousness, everything is permissible and consequences are not even possible. And there may still be pain and anger and sadness, but this happens for nobody, and so it doesn't *matter* anymore (since there's simply nobody here to whom it *could* possibly matter!). There's pain and anger and sadness, but they don't belong to anyone. And so, since nobody is claiming them, they just dissolve of their own accord, in their own time.

And everything being talked about here is *already* the case, for all of us (and yes, that includes "you", of course!). Already, there is liberation. Already, there is freedom from it all. Truly, right now, there is nothing more to attain. Thoughts arise, sounds arise, sights arise, feelings in the body arise, but they always already arise for nobody.

And this may be noticed, or it may not; it really doesn't make a blind bit of difference. There's nobody there to notice it, anyway. And nobody would "get" anything from noticing this, even if they could.

*

Freed from identification, there is only ever *this*. But really, there is nobody who could ever be free from identification in the first place.

Ah, the divine paradox that isn't really a paradox at all. Don't you just love it?

Who Am I?

I am Jeff. I am not Jeff.

I am nothing, no-thing. I am something.

I exist. I don't exist.

I am not this, not that. I am that, I am this.

I am. Who is?

I-am-ness! Who-am-ness?

*

All of the above is true.

All of the above is false.

Good grief.

Listen: A bird tweets outside.

This happens for no-one.

No bird tweets outside. This happens for someone.

A bird tweets. A no-bird doesn't tweet. Can a no-bird tweet?

A no-bird un-tweets its birdy tweeting. For no-one.

A bird tweets its no-birdy un-tweeting. For me.

No bird. No tweeting. No me. No-thing.

And yet: "TWWWEET! TWWWEET!"

This is undeniable.

"TWWWEET! TWWWEET!",
goes the bird in the garden.

"TWWWEET! TWWWEET!"

This is undeniable.

THIS is undeniable.

THIS is this. Is this.

THIS is. This IS.

This is this.

Just this.

Just this.

I am.

Just this.

"TWWWEET! TWWWEET!"

The Kingdom

The Kingdom of Heaven is spread out over the Earth, and men and women do not see it. And it is precisely because men and women are lost in the dream of individuality that they do not see it.

*

We believe we are people; individuals born into an indifferent and sometimes cruel world in which we must find meaning, purpose, and happiness. And this belief has its place, and you only have to look at the past million or so years of human history to see that, well, it may be a dream, but it's a very convincing dream!

And, lost in the dream, so often we wish we could escape from it, and many of us turn to spirituality – Eastern or Western – which promises so much more than this; some higher, more meaningful dimension of existence, something Godly and pure and wonderful, something peaceful and free of suffering. Something better than this Earthly mess, at any rate!

Perhaps we hear about people who have attained enlightenment, or found God, or experienced a total "loss of self", and we may turn these people into our teachers, our gurus. We want what they have, we long to experience what they experience. They look so happy, so peaceful, so free from human suffering! We may even devote our lives to following them, to worshipping them, to listening to their talks and reading their books twenty-four hours a day.

We may even sell our homes, leave our families and go and meditate on a mountain in India. We may change our names, wear spiritual clothes, eat spiritual food. Renounce the body, deny desires, fast until we are but skin and bone. And all of this, of course, has its place. It's all fine and wonderful. But it won't help to end the search.

Because as long as you're doing *something* to get *somewhere*, you're caught up in the search. As long as you're meditating to reach a peaceful state, you're caught up in the search. As long as you're trying to see everything as "one", everything as connected, everything as a manifestation of God, you're caught up in the search. As long as you want to get rid of the "I", the "ego", the "self", you're caught up in the search. As long as you're trying to "be more present" you're caught up in the search. As long as you're looking to become anything other than what you are, or even trying to "Be what you Are" or "Become what you Are" you're caught up in the search. You're even caught up in the search if you're trying to end the search. Or not.

This is really what's known as a double-bind. You're damned if you do, damned if you don't.

So what do you do when there's nothing you can do?

Good question! Anything that could be suggested would just be another way of maintaining the search. As long as the "I" can do something, its continuity is assured. The "I" will even maintain itself by saying "Well, if there's nothing I can do, I will give up the search!" And it tries desperately to give up the search. And in the meantime, its existence is maintained: an individual (me) is trying to give up the search.

So if there's nothing you can do, or not do, what to do?

Nope. I'm not giving you any answers. The search for answers to your questions is just part of the search.

Can't you see that the "I" – that is, "you" – just loves to ask questions? As long as it is asking questions, its continuity is assured: there is a sense of past, future, individuality. There is a person who has questions, and who will eventually find the answers.

Don't you think that if there were answers to find, you'd have found them by now? Haven't you already been given enough answers? Aren't your bookshelves full of answers, overflowing with them?

You see, the questioning must continue, because the "I" must continue. Answers to your questions have been given over and over again, but the "I" cannot accept these as the real answers, because then the questions would be annihilated, and along with them, the "I" who asks the questions. The questioner arises and dissolves with the questions.

So the "I" *must* continue to ask questions and wait for answers. Its very existence is at stake! And so the great search goes on: "*One day* I will be liberated! *One day* I will be free!"

Why not today? Why not now? And if not now, when?

What answers are you waiting for?

What questions are you asking?

*

Perhaps the futility of all this will be seen through, and you may burst out laughing at the ridiculous knots we tie ourselves in, trying to be free, trying to be liberated. Yes, there is a lot of laughter when the dream of individuality and the struggle to be free from it all is seen through, a lot of humour. And perhaps this will happen, and perhaps it won't. But there's nothing "you" can do about it.

*

This "self", this "you", does not have to be denied, or rejected. The search is fine too, the burden of individuality and the longing to be free from it all. The Kingdom of Heaven is indeed spread out over the Earth, and men and women do not see it, but even that – even our ignorance of the Kingdom, even our search for the Kingdom – even that is part the Kingdom. Indeed, there is nothing that the Kingdom is not.

It embraces everything. *Everything*.

Liberation is Paying the Gas Bill

Only this.

Only ever this.

Arising spontaneously.

Leaving no trace.

How could it be otherwise?

Emptiness and fullness, being and non-being.

All is here. All is Now.

But those are just words.

No words necessary.

Just this.

*

Cat miaowing. Kettle on the boil. Heart beating. Eating cornflakes (milk's a bit sour). Bills plopping through the letterbox.

Breathing.

Breathing.

Liberation.

Eating.

Liberation.

Drinking.

Liberation.

Going to the toilet.

Liberation.

Pain in the chest.

Liberation.

Craving, delusion, desire, love, hate, jealously, guilt.

Liberation, liberation, liberation!

*

No need to search anymore.

Was there ever a past?

Was there ever someone who searched? Someone who suffered and longed to be free from it all?

Someone who believed in anything?

Oh, God! What madness! To want anything other than this...

*

Just stop.

Stop, look and listen:

This is all there is.

There was never anything else.

*

I wonder how much British Gas have charged this month?

Liberation is No-Liberation

The idea of wanting to change, how strange it seems to this apparent individual!

Indeed, no liberation is liberation, liberation is no liberation.

And liberation/no-liberation is just this, here now, as it is. No words necessary, but words are fun. The philosophers exclaim "How the hell can liberation be no liberation, that is a logical contradiction!" and the religionists cry "How dare you say that you are God! Burn at the stake, blasphemer!", and the scientists sneer "Well, you can't prove it objectively, so it's simply not true", and the spiritual seekers go "Of course there's such a thing as enlightenment! Ramana Maharshi was enlightened! J. Krishnamurti was enlightened! Nisargadatta Maharaj was enlightened! You're obviously not enlightened!"

And these days, I just sit back and smile. How wonderful it is to be free from all that nonsense. Though, of course, the nonsense is fine and wonderful and doesn't ever need to be denied.

Beyond intellect, beyond all understanding, beyond self and no-self, beyond liberation or not, it's just this.

Typing these words. Breathing. The sound of the taps dripping. Who cares whether or not there is "such a

thing as liberation" when this moment is so damn....
alive...

The Buddha in a Corner Shop

"Before enlightenment, chop wood and carry water.
After enlightenment, chop wood and carry water."
- Wu Li

One day, I met the Buddha in a corner shop.

I went into a little corner shop on the way home from a day in town. After paying for my bread and milk, I asked the guy at the counter if I could have some change for the washing machine. I gave him two pound coins and he gave me back ten 20p pieces, with a broad smile and a "you're welcome".

Enlightenment is not some future "event" that will leave you in a state of "perfection". No – enlightenment happens in each and every moment. It is the simple joy of everyday interactions. It is the buying of bread and milk, the exchange of coins here and there, the "thanks, bye!" as you leave a shop. It's just that, and nothing more.

You cannot "find" enlightenment – at no point can you "become" enlightened. Enlightenment simply IS, and in searching for it, you lose it (although it can never really be lost).

Enlightenment in a corner shop – who would have ever guessed?

Things

Apparently – we are told – there are *things*.
A table. A teapot. A cat. A chair.

Apparent things. All over the place.

Lots of them.

But to whom are these things apparent?

To whom do these things appear?

To me?

And what is "me"?

Is "me" a thing too?

Another thing amongst all these other things?

Can I see a "me"?

Can I smell it, taste it, hear it?

No… But I can feel it. I think.

Yes, it certainly feels like there is a "me".

But to whom does this feeling appear?

Ah.

Ah, I see what you're getting at.

Shit.

Paradox.

Don't like paradoxes.

Wait.

Don't think. See.

Right now. See.

Okay.

The feeling of "me" appears.

To whom does it appear?

To me?

No. The "me" is the feeling that appears.

Yes, yes.

The "me" appears.

It does not appear to "me". It just appears.

That's it. It appears to nobody!

No, no… not even that. "Nobody" is just another idea that appears.

Yes, the "me" just appears!

"I" just appear!

It's just another thing that appears!

A table. A teapot. A cat. A chair. "Me". The plip-plop of the rain outside.

All appearing, spontaneously. Now, now and now.

And now….

Yes, it's just another thing appearing….

…out of nothing?

Out of no-thing?

No, don't need to complicate it.

It's simple:

The "I" appears.

*

So who is writing this?

Shit.

Good one.

Erm…

Hello?

Oh dear. Surely it's *me* who's writing this?

Crap.

Er, wait. Wait. Calm down. Come back to what is obviously the case.

Okay.

Words appear.

Yes, let's start from there.

Fingers move over keys. Doing their little keyboard dance. Tippity-tap!

Yes, the words appear. No need to deny that.

But …. am "I" writing these words?

That's the big question.

Need to find the answer.

*

No, wait.

Of course. "I" don't need to find the answer!

"I" IS the answer. The "I" is the answer!

Oh, it's a vicious circle. Like a dog chasing its tail:

The "I" that seeks is the "I" that is sought.

No need to search for the answer!

THIS is the answer!

Good, good.

Okay.....so, am I writing this?

Well....

Yes and no. Yes, I am writing this. And no, I am not writing this.

Ah, language. Don't you just love it? It's one great big paradox.

No escape from the paradox.

What to do when you cannot escape from a paradox?

You see through the paradox.

Or, more correctly, the paradox is seen through.

*

Words, words, and more words …

The reality is utterly, utterly simple. Utterly obvious.

Look.

Apparently, there are things.

A table. A teapot. A cat. A chair. A "me".

A "me" writing these words, and looking for answers. Or not.

Yes, apparent things. Lots of them. All over the place.

And they all just … happen.

Appear. Arise.

Spontaneously.

A spontaneous play of the divine.

Without beginning or end.

And "I" am both at the centre of it…

…. and nowhere to be found.

Fully present, fully absent.

It doesn't matter.

There's nothing I can do, or not do, about it.

The play goes on.

Liberation is Staring
You in the Face

The morning sun rises, bathing the trees and flowers and birds in a warm, golden glow. What a glorious reminder (although, of course, no reminder is needed) that there is simply nothing to attain. Nowhere to go, nothing to do.... and nobody here who knows any of that.

"Nothing to attain". Yes, I struggled with that for a while! Little old me, always striving for that ultimate awakening experience; one that would, well, "finish things off." The cake wasn't enough – I wanted the icing! But one day, apparently, the need for enlightenment simply dropped. And what is left, I have no way of knowing. There is only *this*; and any idea of "this" just dissolves.

Liberation in each and every moment. Awakening in each and every moment. And nobody here to know it! Nobody to experience it! Nobody at all!

*

I guess the "final hurdle" (and there are no hurdles) was really this: to be enlightened from the need to be enlightened, to awaken from the need to awaken. And the reason I could never "get it" is because, well, "I" was trying to.

It's like trying not to breathe. Hopeless.

*

There is only ever this – what is clearly given in the moment. Sound of keys tapping. Breathing. Slight pain in back. The whirr of the computer fan. Bills piling up on the kitchen table. Voices, faces, noise, heat. Just that! That's IT!

Who would have thought enlightenment was *this*? That the very "thing" we spend our lives searching for is here all along, literally under our noses, literally staring us in the face?

Truly, everything is a manifestation of unconditional love. It is all One Mind, it's all God, it is Nirvana, it is Consciousness, Oneness, The Kingdom of Heaven (call it what you will) – ALL of it. The sacred and the profane, the living and the dying, the fear, the guilt, the pain, the compassion, beheadings in Iraq, mass starvation, bodies being ravaged by cancer, the search for enlightenment, the frustration at "not getting it", paying the bills, feeding the cat, stroking the cat, being bitten by the cat, EVERYTHING! (Okay, so I could do without being bitten by the cat....)

Oh – to experience life, to experience it ALL, in all its magnificence, with no concept of what it should be!

It's pure, unconditional love, all of it. Nothing is excluded.

And it's just this.

And it's astonishing.

And it's so utterly, utterly ordinary.

Everyday life IS liberation, and nothing more needs to be said.

Dialogues I

Q. I don't get it – am I supposed to stop seeking or not? On the one hand you say that seeking is the problem, on the other hand you say that there is nobody there who can seek for anything anyway.

A. Ah, good question. Well, if seeking happens, it happens, and if it doesn't, it doesn't. It's that simple, really. No need to reject seeking, or anything else. If there's pain, there's pain, if there's frustration, there's frustration. It's all just happening right now, a divine show playing out in awareness. And awareness is not separate from this show – not at all.

What tends to happen, though, is that when all of this is seen through (by no-one!) the show or movie (call it what you will – it's just *this*) kind of loses its charge, and there arises a deep and unshakeable sense of okayness with everything that arises, a sense of ease, a sense of "Well, whatever happens, happens". So, if seeking happens... well, who cares! (Literally!) Though paradoxically, as seeking is seen through, it perhaps tends to happen less and less.

But of course, "you" cannot stop seeking, that would just be more seeking (seeking the end of seeking!). Fun, yes?

The nonduality marketplace certainly appears to be riddled with these kinds of paradoxes, eg. there is a seeker / there is no seeker, giving up the search is possible / giving up the search is more of the search, and so on. But who is aware of these paradoxes? And who is trying to overcome them? You see, it's so simple. The paradoxes are there – let's not deny them. But already they arise now, already they arise for no-one. Already, the paradoxes are resolved, so there's no need to seek for any sort of resolution in the first place. Still, if seeking happens, that's fine.

Does reading about Advaita or going to talks by non-dual teachers, etc, help to end the search?

This apparent individual hardly ever listens to or reads about this "stuff" these days. I've gone back to reading fiction novels and taking walks in the park! Life is simple and ordinary. Not that there's anything wrong with reading books and listening to talks. But there might be the subtle belief that you're going to "get" something from the talks, that they can give you a bit of a "lift" or make you feel a little more "clear" or "relax the sense of I" a bit more, or make you more "aware". So there's still that subtle goal, that subtle seeking....

Is there something somehow "wrong" with seeking and being frustrated at not "getting it"?

No, there absolutely does not need to be any end to seeking or anything else that arises. The seeking is fine, the frustration is fine. But what has become apparent over here is that when the seeking is seen through (by no-one) it becomes blindingly clear that seeking was always the "problem". In other words, as long as I (apparently) was seeking, there was frustration; there was the idea of some "goal" that could be attained in the future, some enlightened or liberated "state" that was somehow different from *this*. There was a deep frustration and unease at "not getting it".

These days, all that seeking has dropped (been seen through) and there is a deep sense of ease, an ease which always has been here, but perhaps was obscured, in the past, by my (apparent) incessant seeking. Undoubtedly, the search is frustrating!

I'm not saying "Drop the search", because the effort to do that would just be a prolonging of the search. I'm not even saying "Accept the search", because the effort to accept the search would again just be more of the same. Time and time again people tell me that they are "waiting" for the search to end. But this "waiting" is merely more seeking. We seek the end of seeking, and then we wonder why we haven't "got it" yet!

We haven't got it yet simply because there's nothing to get! As long as we're waiting to "get it", the search goes on. Which is all absolutely fine, really. As I've said, rejecting the search would just be *more* of the search.

For some reason we kid ourselves that seeking the end of seeking isn't "really" seeking!

How does religion fit into what we're talking about? I don't understand, is there someone there who can even choose to be religious, or not? Or am I just being picky about paradoxes?

All there is, is this, and if thoughts about religion (and this includes the religion of atheism!) arise, well, that too is part of this divine play. And it's all fine and absolutely wonderful, but it has absolutely nothing to do with liberation. Because nothing you can do – and that includes religion and its various beliefs and practices

– can bring you any closer to *this*. Because *this* (look around you!) is always already the case. Always.

Absolutely, the apparent "you" can still pretend to follow religions, can still meditate, can still take the kids to the zoo, can still watch trashy TV programmes (*X Factor* included). It's all part of the play. The play includes everything!

And you're right, we could pick at the apparent paradoxes until we're blue in the face. But isn't that just more of the search? "Once I resolve the paradoxes, once I understand this better, I'll be free...." and so on, and so on. It just prolongs the search, and with it, the individual who searches. All wonderful again, but totally, totally unnecessary. Because *this* is all there is, all there ever has been, and all there ever will be.

It's always here, it's always now, it's always this. Religion or no religion, belief or no belief, just this.....

I still feel that seeking is a problem. For example, a big thing with me is "seeking the end of the self"....

Well yes, I hear you! I too (apparently) used to want to "be rid of the self". This of course is now seen to be utterly futile, because of course only a self would seek for the end of self!

I used to believe that I could seek my way to liberation. It is now seen (by no-one) that liberation is always already here... and it is the seeking which implies it is not. So, for the individual ("me"), absolutely, seeking IS the problem, the self IS the problem (otherwise, why would there be seeking? Seeking implies that there is something wrong with NOW, with THIS, and there could be something better in the future).

But this individuality, this seeking, this self, this "I" does not need to be denied. It simply arises in the play of life. It's all wonderful. It just happens... for no-one.

So where does that leave us? Once seeking falls away, what is left? Well, the answer is staring you in the face. And it's utterly ordinary, simple, and obvious. Liberation is just this, now: thoughts arising, self arising, feelings in the body arising, sounds arising, smells arising. Just this! And we spend our whole lives searching for something else!

I think I get this, and I think I've pretty much given up the search, but one thing puzzles me. It's about control: am I in control of all this or not? It certainly seems that way sometimes....

Well, it seems like you're still looking for an "answer", waiting to "get it". What I've "discovered" I guess (and it's not really a discovery at all) is that there really *is* no answer, and it's only when we're searching for one that we get really confused. If there was an answer to all this, don't you think you'd have found it by now? Could it be that there's no real answers, but only the questions? Could it be that the questions just stem from this feeling of incompleteness, a dissatisfaction with the present life? Could the questions just be a symptom of the longing to escape this life?

Just come back to what is: breathing, sensations in the

body, thoughts passing through, noises in the room. What does it really matter who is in control of all this? You could go round in circles trying to find out (and believe, me, I did! We all do!). Just notice: it all happens. No matter what you do, or don't do, it's all just happening now. Spontaneously.

And then the question "Who is in control of this? I don't understand!" bubbles up. That's when the trouble begins, that's the search rearing its head. It's only when I (apparently) dropped the search for something other than this – this moment, awareness and its passing content (which really are not separate) – that this ease and calm started to appear; an ease and calm that had been there all along, but had been obscured by my incessant search for answers to it all.

You don't need theories about creating your life, about whether things happen with or without belief, or with or without personal control; that is still all mental, all thought. Just come back to what is: it's all happening, presently. Nothing more is needed. This moment is all there is. This moment is the answer. Any question implies that you need a future to find an answer.

So you may start to notice how the mind's function really is to prove how "This moment isn't enough! I want something ELSE!!! I want something MORE!" You may start to see through the futility of that.

Wanting liberation is still a want, like any other, no matter what we want to believe!

By offering these "teachings" aren't you implying

that you are separate from the people you are "teaching"? Aren't you supposed to be "nondual"? Doesn't this separation imply duality?

Of course. But even conversing with each other like this assumes some sort of separation: someone talking to someone else. We have to use the *idea* of separation to function sanely and intelligently in this world. We have to use language (which implies separation, duality) to ask for a loaf of bread, to ask for directions to the M60.

We can play with duality but we do not have to believe in it. Then life regains its joy: to see it all as a cosmic game, a play. Not to deny the duality, but to embrace it. Nirvana is samsara. This ordinary life *is* enlightenment, *is* the Kingdom of Heaven.

Seeing everything as "not separate" is just another thought, another belief. All of which means, when someone comes up to me to ask for help, yes, duality is an illusion, if we want to use those words, but the idea of "you and me" still arises, and it does not have to be denied or rejected. The idea of separation is fine as it is. To see it as that – just an idea, just an appearance – is what we might call freedom.

On a practical level, I can still interact with people, completely normally. On a practical level, there are still two bodies, one over here and one over there. I can still talk to you, *as if* you were a separate person. And that is the great mystery – the divine paradox: there is no "you" and no "me", but apparently there *is*! We don't have to reject the "you and me"; we don't have to reject our humanity. Just to see it is enough. To see it is to end it.

And to end it is just this: "Hi Tom, how are you?!" In reality, there is no Tom, and no "me" saying hello. But still, life goes on, and Tom and I have a wonderful conversation. Nothing has to be denied: real spirituality is just everyday life, as it is.

So yes, of course there is the *idea* of separation. But ultimately it is nothing more than that.

Aren't you just another "therapist", another "reliever of suffering"?

I am whatever you say I am! (If I wasn't, then why would I say I am?)

Apologies for the Eminem reference there. To answer your question, I'm absolutely not setting myself up as a reliever of suffering. I hope it doesn't appear that way! If someone came to me and said they were upset and they wanted help, I would perhaps try to help them, because in their eyes, they are suffering. In my eyes, all suffering is an illusion (because it assumes that there is an individual there who can actually suffer), but they apparently cannot see this yet. I know, because once in my life I suffered intensely, and if someone had told me back then that all suffering was an illusion, I'd have told them where to shove their spiritual crap!

To be honest, I don't really do "therapy" at all. If "therapy" happens, it is unplanned; it just spontaneously happens in the moment. If someone is there in front of me, asking for help, I may (or may not) help them, I don't really have any choice in the matter! If I set myself up as some sort of healer, what a hypocrite

I would be. What arrogance, to assume that I "had the answers" and that others weren't perfect as they are! Everybody *is* perfect just as they are; the thing is that a lot of people don't see this yet. And for those people, it may appear that someone like me could help them. And if they ask for help, I might (or might not) help them. I have no idea.

All I know is that in the past, some things I have said to some people may have helped them. Or not. Perhaps just being in the presence of someone who is listening without comment, or who doesn't see a problem; perhaps that is worth something to some people. I don't know.

It's like with the Buddha; his teachings are for those who have not "realised" yet. The teachings are still part of the delusion, but they may be a "helpful" part of the delusion, that may help to "end" delusion, or not. And no, I'm not comparing myself to the Buddha! Except I do have a rather round belly these days....!

Not that I am condemning suffering. Suffering is a necessary part of life. Until you realise that it probably isn't. Because, ultimately, there is nobody there who suffers. And this may be seen, or not. There's nothing to be "gained" by seeing it, not at all.

Are you holding consciousness in the palm of your hand? Able to play with it, like a toy?

Sounds nice!

People believe that once they "awaken" (and there is no such thing) they will be able to use consciousness in some way, but is this not just another desire? The desire to get something, and use it to one's advantage? Does this desire not maintain the search, and with it, the separate self-sense? Isn't this just a very subtle, sneaky way for the search to continue? Consciousness is That which you already are, and any attempt to "use" consciousness is consciousness attempting to use itself.

Beyond this paradox of words, beyond all mind-created ideas and ideals of enlightenment, consciousness and awakening, who are you? Who is aware of these words? Who is not already enlightened?!

I'm confused, I've heard if something is meant to happen it will because it can't be any other way. But to me that implies a destiny.

Well, yes, "meant to happen" would imply a destiny, some sort of future for this individual that is planned out in some way. But those are just words, concepts, thoughts, beliefs, mind stuff, and they all go towards maintaining the sense of the individual entity.

In reality, we cannot know the future. Thoughts about the future, projections and predictions and stories about what will happen arise, but they arise now. They are only thoughts arising now. Thoughts of "having a destiny", thoughts of "what will happen", thoughts of "self" arise too, and those are just thoughts. And they all arise in *this*.

And it's true, you could say "What will happen will happen", but that's almost like saying nothing at all!

The point is, you cannot know what will happen, not even in the next moment. All of that is just a story arising now. "Destiny" is always a story, a thought, a belief arising now. Meanwhile, the clarity and aliveness which is already fully present, is apparently ignored, and turned into a goal, something to reach in the future.

There is no destiny, no future, only *this*. It's the most obvious thing, so simple that we may overlook it our whole lives. Or not!

Help! This is all so confusing. There are so many teachers, so many people saying apparently different things...

Yes, the so-called nonduality marketplace can be rather confusing to an individual trying to get somewhere! So many things to worry about: *Is there any such thing as a "purely nondual" teaching? Are some teachings "better" than others? Should we "stay away" from so-called "dualistic teachings"? Even people like Tony Parsons – he still has "meetings" and apparently "answers questions" – isn't this very subtly promoting the idea of duality, the idea that there is "something to get"?*

Yikes indeed!

The answer? This! Who is it, right now, that is confused? Who is it that may be trying to "get" something from these so-called teachings (or non-teachings!)? Is that sense of "me" arising now? Good. Nothing more is needed. That's IT. I mean it. That's IT. Liberation is JUST this: sun shining through the window, thoughts bubbling up from nowhere, sense of "me" arising and dissolving, cat screaming for food, hunger for lunch arising.... just this......

... and then the thought *"this can't be it!!!"* – that's the killer!

Ah, dear old "me", dear old mind. Always wanting something more. Always looking for something other than this.

What about personal or individual choice? Since there is no "I" to have any choice, it's all just happening, right? So there's nothing I can do? That sounds very depressing....

Ah, choice ... the old chestnut! You see, "There is no choice" and "There is a choice" are both beliefs; both necessarily arise together and dissolve together. Beyond both, there is just *this* .... no belief necessary. No choice or lack of choice, just this. Here. Now. Utter, utter simplicity. Utter, utter obviousness.

Clinging onto "There is no choice" is just as dualistic as any other teaching. In fact, I'd say that in the world of individuality, in which we all must function whether we like it or not (we all woke up and got dressed this morning, we will all eat and drink today), I'd say that "There is no choice" can be a very depressing and frankly life-denying belief. Plenty of people get very depressed because they believe they have no choice!

Nonduality is not about denying anything. We don't need to deny apparent choice, nor apparent preferences, nor apparent suffering, nor apparent good and evil. But all of this ceases to have a mesmerising effect once it is seen through. It just arises in the infinite space that we are. The space is big enough for all of it. None of it has to be denied.

It's all a miracle – it's all the play of the divine. Choice or no choice – no need to cling to either polarity. I think that's what so-called "nondual teachers" are pointing to when they say "There is no choice, no individual, no volition". Words are definitely very misleading! But then, of course, it's never about the words.

So why is there such a big fuss about "enlighten-ment" and "enlightened people" then? I mean, if it's all a futile search?

You know, liberation, awakening, enlightenment... it's really all one big joke! There is only ever *this*, and nobody here to experience it.... just the passing of content through awareness.... now, now, and now.....

As for people who claim to be enlightened... they are just people who are walking around with the belief "I am enlightened, and other people are not". This is just another belief, another story arising in awareness.

If there are any "enlightened people" (and it's a contra-diction in terms) you would never, ever know, because they would appear to be completely ordinary, com-pletely normal. And they themselves would have no way of knowing either; the concept of an enlightened person would be utterly meaningless to them. If peo-ple go round telling the world they are enlightened, this is just another ego-trip, no different from telling everyone that they are "the king of pop" or "the people's princess" or "a great and powerful leader". It's just another story, another identity, another belief. Another way to separate one human being from another. Another act of violence.

Beware of people who go round claiming to be enlightened! I speak from experience: for a while, believe it or not, I used to believe I was enlightened. These days, all that nonsense has been seen through. There is ONLY this, here, now, and claiming to be enlightened is just another way to maintain a strong individual self-sense...

Forget any ideas about enlightenment or liberation: THIS IS IT. Nothing else is needed..... just this. A bird sings, the heart beats, the computer fan hums, the traffic roars outside: it's all just a play, a game, a wonderful show. There is no such thing as liberation, because liberation is *this*, and it cannot be a thing or a goal or something to achieve in the future, because a goal would imply a "me", and right now, "me" is just a thought arising in *this*. But that's all fine and wonderful. Nothing needs to be denied.

I seem to be obsessed with looking for an answer. Is the answer to not look for an answer?

Well, looking for an answer may happen or not. When the search is on, there may be tension, frustration, a sense that there is something to get in the future. When the search relaxes, when there is no longer a strong sense of "looking for an answer", there is a sense of ease, and an "okayness" with things as they are.... with no real worry as to how things could be in the future.

Looking for an answer can't be the answer, because it implies that *this*, here, now, is not the answer, that liberation is somewhere in the future. But liberation is always already here – it is just this, at it is.... breathing...reading these words.... looking for an answer, or not. Just that is the only answer there is. It is, indeed, the "open secret", always already present... no search necessary!!

And then of course, the mind goes "But this can't be it!!!" ... and the search goes on. But that's all fine and wonderful too...

Here, there seems to be the desire to "fix" things. But I know that's just more seeking. How is it for you?

Well yes….. I spent most of my life locked in the idea that "I" was not good enough, and therefore "I" needed to be made better somehow. Then, in my early 20's, I got all "spiritual" and believed that I'd only be free when I actually got rid of the "I" and became enlightened, like all those so-called Buddhas I'd read about!

These days, all of this is seen through, and it makes me laugh out loud sometimes when I think of all the ridiculous demands I was putting on myself. And so many of the teachings I was following were teachings of imprisonment, because they spoke to a "me" who could do something to get free….

There's simply nobody here to fix, and nobody here who'd want to be fixed anyway. Why would anyone want to fix *this*? This moment is the answer to all and any questions. Just this.

And what is so astonishing about all of it is that while, in actuality, there is no entity, no doer, no individual, there is, most definitely, an apparent entity, an apparent doer, an apparent individual. It's all a great appearance, a great show, but *when we look closely, there's simply nothing there.* That's the divine paradox: there is nothing, and apparently there is something. There is nothing, but there are things.

This world is an apparent world, a song-and-dance of a world, a great play, and when that is seen (by nobody) it somehow all takes on a strange beauty, because its just not *serious* any more. How could a play be serious? A play has no purpose but itself!

And with that "discovery" comes a great deal of ease and humour, and a sense of "okayness" about the whole damn thing. I used to think I'd come into this world to "find my purpose" as they say. Now, it is seen: THIS is the only purpose. THIS is the beginning and end of it all, the Alpha and the Omega. THIS is it. Damn strange!

I still feel that there is something to be discovered. It feels frustrating.

Yes – sometimes there can be frustration at not "getting it" yet. But can you see, seeking not to seek is just more seeking! It involves a future goal – the goal that says "One day, I'll be one of those people who don't seek anymore".

Can you see that this yearning to no longer seek is just a way for seeking (and with it a strong sense of self as a "seeker") to continue?

What happens if seeking is just allowed to arise, and it is not condemned? What happens if seeking-an-end-to-seeking is simply seen through?

Do thoughts of seeking arise now, in this moment? Do thoughts of "I just don't get it" or "I haven't yet recognised my true nature" arise?

And what about the thought "I shouldn't be having these thoughts anymore!" Is that arising now?

You see, these thoughts just arise, and the secret is that they may always arise. There will always be thought. Don't believe those who claim they've ended thought: only thought would claim to have ended thought! And trying to get rid of thought is just more thought!

Thought is fine, as it is, because *already* it arises for nobody. It simply arises in awareness. There is nobody there "having" those thoughts: that's the illusion.

This is always already the case – nothing more needs to be done. So let's go down the pub!

Nope. Still confused. Don't get it at all.

Well, this is the simplest of messages. There's really nothing to "get". The idea that there's something special to "get" is what will keep you (apparently) on the merry-go-round. It can be very frustrating for an individual (that is, "you") to believe there's something to "get"!

In this moment, there is thought arising... there are

noises.... the beating of the heart.... breathing.....per-haps the thought "I'm confused, this can't be it!"... the taps dripping.... the hum of cars outside.....

Nothing more is needed. Seeking is fine. And seeking an end to seeking is just more seeking!

The answer to all your questions is this moment, as it is.

Now it's *definitely* time to go down the pub...

PART TWO

Realising There's Nobody Home

*"Listen to your life. See it for the fathomless mystery that
it is. In the boredom and pain of it no less than in the
excitement and gladness: touch, taste, smell your way to
the holy and hidden heart of it because in the last analysis
all moments are key moments,
and life itself is grace."*

— Frederick Buechner

The Dance of Form

And so it dawns on me: the realisation that each and every moment is unfolding as it should. There are no errors. There is no luck. No chance. No cause or effect. There is only this – ineffable, impenetrable, unspeakable this – at once both comically unreal, and as shockingly vivid as a punch to the stomach. How could I have not seen this?

This is inexplicable, inexpressible. This is God, One-ness, Absolute Reality, Consciousness, Spirit, manifest and unmanifest, emptiness and form. And it is all One, and all is well. There is not a thing out of place, for if it was, who would know it? There is nothing to be achieved, for if there was, who would achieve?

Atoms and mountains and oceans and light, all aris-ing, dissolving, arising again. The dance of form which is really the dance of emptiness; a dance which is the beginning and end of all things. In each moment there is creation and destruction, in each moment a new Kosmos arises and dissolves, leaving no trace. And this continues endlessly, without beginning, without end.

"Oh, lost souls, can't you see you are all Gods?"

Nothing Wrong with Silence

This is the unnameable Mystery. And yet we give it a name.

And having named the unnameable Mystery a thousand times over, we take those names to be the reality. And we live according to that reality, forgetting that the names were arbitrary, and a product of the mind.

And the names torture us; we are caught in the middle of the polarities, torn between the opposites: good and evil, love and hate, right and wrong, rich and poor, ugly and beautiful, sacred and profane. This prison is of our own making, and yet we do not realise we do it to ourselves.

The mind (that is, "you") is not interested in the Mystery, because the mystery cannot be an object of knowledge. Indeed, it is That from which objects of knowledge arise, the Void which gives birth to all life. Without it there is nothing. Call it the Tao, call it God, call it Spirit, call it Consciousness, call it Life, call it nothing at all or even deny it; even the denial of it is simply It denying itself. No proof is needed for It. Why? Because this moment is. You are here. It is now. That, and just that, is God. There is no need for belief.

A belief in God is a denial of God. You don't need to believe in something if that something is staring you in the face!

*

And when this is realised, how quiet everything becomes! All mental noise dies away, and is seen for what it is: a false reality, an illusion, nothing more. You are no longer a person: not a man, not a woman, not English, not American, not black, not white, not Hindu, not Christian, not Muslim, not atheist, not rich or poor, good or bad, not happy or sad; you are not any of these things; you are not this, not that, not any object of consciousness. You are not the body, not the mind. Those feet are not yours, those hands, those legs. That face doesn't belong to you. That head is there, but you do not own it. No eyes, no tongue, no nose, no throat, no heart. No form. Before you are all of these things, you are. You are consciousness. You are awareness. Pure, unconditioned awareness. Not the idea but the actuality, the simple feeling of being. Presence.

You are Life itself, not an individual cut off from the whole, but you are one with all things, because all things are manifestations of the one Life, and you are that Life. The illusion of individuality arises, yes – but it is a manifestation, and you are not doing it. It is not personal. And the manifestation need not be denied – no, it is there. No self-denial is necessary.

The self arises. Let it be. It is an illusion, after all, a construction of thought. You are prior to that construction, you are the awareness in which the construction arises. You are the awareness in which the "you" arises. This is not clever wordplay but the actuality of things – look for yourself right now. Meditate on it. Come back to present experience (this is true meditation). Is there anything solid there called "self"? Is there any clear distinction between you and not you? Where is the boundary? Are "you" contained within the skin surrounding the body? Is that what you experience yourself as?

Come back to the present experience! Without reference to the past, can you know who you are? Can you say who you are, really?

*

Ah, this is tiring. Attempting to name the unnameable, to describe that which is prior to all description. Perhaps I should just let it be.

There is nothing more to say. Silence is the only honest way to go. Once you reach this point all words are just noise. Noise to fill the silence which is prior to, and envelops, all noise. Why do we pay so much attention to the noise? What is wrong with silence?

*

Silence.

We reach the point of creation.

Why is there anything at all?

Why isn't there Nothing?

What is wrong with silence?

*

The noise comes, though. But now we see it in a new way. It is pointless. In the sense that it is equal to silence. Not better, not worse. But it is undeniably there. So we honour it; we do not deny it.

And so now life becomes a play, a game, a divine dance, because it's all meaningless and pointless and purpose-less, and it exists for no reason whatsoever other than to be itself. Noise and silence, noise and silence, insepara-ble. Being and non-being, inseparable. Me and not-me, inseparable. Everything in divine union, not fragments anymore but aspects of a whole, each part important, each piece enabling everything else to be; nothing out of place, nothing unwanted, nothing disposable. Noth-ing sacred, nothing profane. Being and non-being as two aspects of consciousness, as the two faces of God. And really, God has no faces at all.

Ah, but the words are just ripples on the surface. Plunge back into the silence. No words needed. No words necessary.

No real urge to speak of it anymore. Just the simple feeling of being is enough, the simplicity of this, just this. This moment.

*

Only this. Only ever this.

Why did it take so long to see it? Why was I sleepwalk-ing my whole life?

It doesn't matter now. Let the past slide away. It is as unreal as the imagined future.

The sound of breathing. The hum of the computer. The creaking of the radiator. A tingling in the toes. Hands moving over keys. Words coming out. Breathing. A sense of deep peace. This is *life*, damn it! Here! Right here!

Words cannot even scratch the surface of things. And yet we spend our lives scratching on the surface. Thinking we have the answers. Not realising that there are no answers, because there are no questions. There were never any questions, because this moment is always already perfect the way it is. Any question would take you away from that.

Oh, let it be. Let it all be.

*

Stay rooted in the silence, and honour the noise…

Disintegration – 3 a.m.

No world outside; only *this*.

Now the words don't come, and now they do.

No control over this. Spontaneous.

It breathes, it breathes. No reason to breathe, no reason to stop.

No words for this; all words arise into this, and dissolve into this.

Nothing remains. No trace, no track, no memory.

All answers dissolve, all questions dissolve; all just energy arising, energy falling away.

*

Now thought does not come.

Mind is clear, like the sky. An open space.

No clouds. Only silence, only space, only this.

Cars outside. Water through pipes. Banging upstairs. The forms arise and pass, leaving no trace. Any trace is memory, any trace is dead.

Words that do not do this justice: peace, God, emptiness, nirvana, freedom. Who would want to describe this anyhow?

All philosophies fail here. This cannot be captured. This cannot be reduced. Then what is being written? Nothing. This means nothing. But it is being written! There is nothing, there is something. Identical!

Nothing, something. Something, nothing. Duality, nonduality. Nonduality, duality.

All is clear. There never was any confusion. Confusion is illusion.

Did I ever think otherwise?

*

So what to do? When there is nothing to do, what to do?

Do what you do! That is all.

What am I doing now? Writing. Why? Because I am. No other reason. Nothing else is possible. Only this. What freedom in that; what liberation! Nothing else is possible but this. This moment. And this. To fight that – to demand that this be something other than what is – is madness. Total madness. Total futility. This is perfect, simply because it can't be any other way.

No illusions. No illusion of control. There is no control, nor lack of it. Thoughts of control and lack of control both arise; they both fall away. Only this remains. And this, and this, endlessly......

*

Is this the "great liberation"? There is only that question. And the question signifies nothing. No answer is assumed, and the question dissolves back into nothingness – the nothingness that IS total fullness. Nothing and something are one.

*

Duality? Nonduality? Nonsense. God? A fancy story. Nirvana? A dream, no more, no less. All these concepts arise and fall back into the perfection that is this moment, and this moment, and this.

*

Is this a "state"? Who asks the question? Is an answer assumed? Is the answer in the question? Is the answer the question itself?

So let the question dissolve back into the emptiness.....

This. This. Only this. Forever, endlessly, timelessly, without beginning, without end. Older than God. Prior to eternity.

*

Past is memory. Future is projection. Neither exist ... or don't exist.

*

Language is circular. There is nothing to convey. Why do we talk? To convey! But there is nothing to convey! And that is the great liberation. We talk because we do. It is the assumption that there is something to convey that is the confusion! We talk because we talk, and when we don't, we don't. And that's it. There is nothing outside of that.

Language is circular, and until we see language for what it is, we are trapped in it. Language cannot take us to where we already are. It cannot point outside of itself. Language arises in this moment, and that is fine. If there is no language, that too is fine. But language will never capture this, because it is smaller than this. Everything, that is, every concept, is smaller than this – a mere drop in the infinite ocean that is this.

So why do anything at all? This is the great Perfection, and yet I am apparently *doing* something. Except there is no I! "I" would just be a thought arising in this moment – and that is fine – but it is an illusion that this "I" can control anything, in this moment or any other!

"I" am not typing this. There is typing. And thought arises "I am typing this". That is all. And the typing continues. And another thought arises. But there is nothing there. No self. No lack of self. No self to find, no self to lose. No self-discovery. No extinction of self, no search. All searches unravel in this.

*

No world outside. All world is here. Typing, typing. This is the world. No world outside.

Breathing, breathing. Silence. How perfectly it all unfolds, moment to moment.

No control. The body breathes, right on cue. The eyes blink, right on cue. The fingers type, each hitting its key at the perfect moment. Nobody here to control them.

Hello? Anyone home?

Who is asking? Who is typing?

"What is the self"? – who asks? The answer asks! The assumed answer! But the question must die, the moment it is asked. It is false, built on a lie, a fallacy. It assumes an answer! The question and the search for the answer arise at the same time. Where there is a question, there is the assumption of an answer, and there is a search, a contraction of this. The question kills this. Unless it is seen. Seen!

"What is the self?" Four words and a question mark! That is ALL. No answer. No answer. And so no question, and no search. And it brings you back to THIS, which was here all along, which IS here all along, at this moment. The question IS the moment, in its totality, the moment it is asked. Why do you search for an answer to the question, when the question simply unravels in the moment?

*

A question is identical with the assumption of an answer.

What is the nature of reality? – this assumes a nature of reality. What is the self? – this assumes a self. What is Ultimate Truth? – this assumes Ultimate Truth.

*

To see the world as it really is – and not how one thinks it is – that is freedom.

No philosophy will get you here. No self-help guide. No teacher, no way of thinking. No meditation. No prayer, no charity, no love, no nothing. You cannot get here because you are already here. To search for this implies you haven't found it yet. But you have found it; it is right under your nose. It is your nose. And everything else! How can you find yourself when you are yourself? Can an eyeball see itself? The seer can see everything except the seer! You will never find this, because you are this! And this! And this!

*

This is never the same. Only your thoughts about this are. Thought is dead. Only this is alive. Eternal life? It's right here, now! Heaven? This!

*

Maybe the body should sleep. But for now, it types. When it stops typing, I expect it will get into bed. I won't mind either way. It does what it does, and I love that it does, because it does!! If it didn't, it wouldn't, and I'm sure I'd love that too, unless I didn't, in which case I wouldn't, and that would be fine too. Unless it wasn't. Hey – this is fun!! This is what it is. In every moment, it is perfectly itself, never claiming to be anything other than what it is. It is pure honesty, pure integrity, pure humility. And it's not serious. There is great humour in this. Great humour. Great release.

*

Why something instead of nothing? Because there IS something. There is a computer in front of me, and there is a curtain, and a mug, and a light. Except the mug is not a mug. It is what it is. We just call it "mug" for purposes of communication. But we really have no idea what it is. *It's a mug – it's not a mug.* Same thing. Equal. It's great that it's a mug. If there were nothing, there wouldn't be a mug, and I wouldn't be talking about it. So, there's a mug. And that's wonderful. Philosophy won't get you here! *It's a mug – it's not a mug.* What difference. Just words. I have no way of knowing what IT is. What THIS is. But we use words – or we don't. It doesn't matter.

Nothing to convey. But we do anyway – because we might as well. No deeper reason.

*

Body tired now. This may be near the end.

Breathing. Silence.

Only this. Forever this, always this. Nothing to fight anymore. Total acceptance, total rejection, total emptiness, total fullness. The clash of the opposites, the tension of the paradoxes, the frustration at "not getting it": everything unravels in this moment.

Freedom, liberation, enlightenment, peace: those are just words. They don't do this justice, and yet, they are all the justice that needs to be done. No compulsion, no control, no end to this. Endlessly, forever, always.

3am, 12ᵗʰ March 2005, Oxford, UK.

The Peace of God

*"Bind me like a seal upon thine heart; love is as
strong as death."*

– Song of Solomon 8:6

God Almighty, everything is empty! I find no basis
for anything; nothing upon which anything can
stand. The world whirls in a vacuum of nothingness,
and I (whatever the hell I am) am not *separate* from that
nothingness.

And we spend our lives resisting this nothingness!
But this nothingness is who we are! And so in fact
we resist ourselves; we resist life, and deny the very
ground of our being, the very ground we walk on! And
this is considered to be normality! And the man who
sees into this nothingness and who tries to express it
in language, this man is the crazy man, the fool, the
schizophrenic, the psychotic…. or the mystic.

How to express nothingness? How to name the
unnameable? Try to talk about it and you assume an
"it" to talk about.

You're fucked if you talk about it, fucked if you don't.

Silence seems to be the only option.

*

Yes, yes. Silence. Let it be. Let it all be. It's all my very
own self, anyhow. All of this.

The world is not "out there" for me to gaze upon; no, the world and I are one. My world is the world is me is myself is I. These words are me and I am these words, and they are not words and I am not me, but apparently there is a me and there are words.

Out there and *in here* are not-two.

Oh, whatever. There's no point even talking about it. Words are part of the problem. To speak about something implies there is something to speak about. It implies someone who is speaking and something spoken. It implies knowledge. It implies past and future. It implies the division of consciousness which is at the root of the human delusion.

Oh, to be free from this delusion! But the one who wants to be free from the delusion is already PART of the delusion, is the delusion itself! No escape is possible!

And really no escape is needed. Embrace it – embrace it all, damn it! Delusion, self, thought, past, future, escape, imprisonment: embrace it, embrace it! And the embracing of it all is death! And to die in this moment is to really live! To drop all thoughts, all preconceptions, all interpretations, and to SEE, with the eyes of a child, with the eyes of a saint. To SEE what is in front of you. To disappear in favour of THIS!

To relax into the moment, which only alone is. Nothing but this. Nothing but this.

Therein lies our salvation. Therein lies the peace of God.

Night-Time Voices

All arises without purpose.

Shapes, forms, images, imaginations, hallucinations, flares and flashes of colour and rhythm and ordered and disordered spirals of infinite complexity dancing and swirling without intention, meaning, value or goal.

It is a dance, and the purpose of the dance is the dance. The dance has no purpose but itself. Its purpose is no purpose. But to grasp this dance, to try to hold it, to keep it, to make it my own – there's the sorrow, there's the suffering. How to grasp the ungraspable?

To grasp the ungraspable one must first un-grasp one's grasp of the graspable.

Yeah, right.

I want to grab you and shake you and wake you up from your slumber. I want to tear your insides out and put them back in back-to-front, so that insides are outsides are insides in one undivided wholeness, so you return to and become the All. And you always have been one with the All, and so there was never anything to become in the first place. Back to the beginning of all things. The Alpha and the Omega, and now cascading down, down into the infinite Abyss from which the Alpha and Omega arose, and to which all things eventually return.

The Abyss will eat everything in the end.

*

I hate these words. I hate them. Black on white. The creation of apparent worlds of form and structure and time and space. Contrast on contrast. Attempting to point beyond themselves, but always ending up pointing back to themselves again.

The finger cannot point to itself. But perhaps I can point to the finger trying to point to itself. Perhaps I can point to the self trying to point the finger.

The whirr of cars outside, the whoosh of the boiler, now the click as it turns off, voices in the street calling to one another (or are they calling to themselves?) and they are all me, and I am all they. Not fragments, not parts, not things, but each thing being also part of another thing, and another thing, and another thing, so no thing is by itself, for itself, of itself, but only a thing in so much as it as a part of a greater thing; and in fact it is only when a thing is a part of a greater thing that it can be called a thing, for a thing is a boundary, and a boundary is a thing, inside torn from outside torn from the All. But the voices call to each other, and it is still night. A thing or not a thing, there are those voices. God calls to himself late at night on a street corner, and nobody hears.

Silence.

What else is needed? Isn't it all just a game to fill the silence? What is there to say, and who would want to say it? And to whom?

The world was always *here*. But the world tricks you, it claims to be "out there". No, no. It was never out there. There were never any things, people, places, events. The dualistic happy-unhappy dream is over, which is to say it never happened. Now there is only breathing which I do not do, and the beat of a heart which I do not have, and the sights and smells and sounds of a room in which I have never been. If the room is anywhere, it is in me. And perhaps, but only perhaps, I am in it.

Words, they point to the clarity but never touch it. Perhaps they touch it at the point they are written. Creation, destruction. Black ink on white background. Nothing happens at all.

No, we are not *people*. Miserable, wretched little people, struggling to make ends meet, working towards our individual egoic goals that remains unreachable as long as we are trying to reach them. No, we are not people, flimsy bags of flesh and bone animated with a divine breath of life, cast out into an unloving world where disease and poverty and hunger and old age wait just beyond the edges of things to snatch away our fun when we least expect. No, we are not people, we who walk along the boundaries of a false reality, caught between the polarities, torn apart by the yes and the no of the world, the single and the multiple, the dual and the nondual, the east and west.

No, we are not people, but we are that which allows people to be in the first place, we are the conditions by which people can know themselves as people. We are not people, but we are *peopling*, and we define ourselves only now, now and now, never stopping to keep a record of what has gone, or projecting what is to come. Lift a rock and you will find us. Open a door and you will find us. Look to the heavens and you will find us. Beyond good and evil, beyond all things, and beyond even that, right at the heart of all phenomena our dance originates, our passion and compassion embracing all forms equally, no one and no thing excepted. Nothing excepted but exception itself. And perhaps not even that.

No, we are not people, but what we are, we will never know.

*

In the end it is all for nothing, this attempt to clarify what is inherently muddled, jumbled, messed up, torn, tattered, fragmented, divided. We are shreds of what we could be, and alienated from what we are. Where do we start when the devastation runs this deep? Perhaps from the beginning. Perhaps we start where we went off course, and work from there. If the world never existed, then we have nothing to lose. Or could this just be another ploy to deepen the devastation? If you have to ask, you are already off course. But the course itself is off course. And there was never any course to leave.

Fuck it. You will remain unmoved. A broken heart needs more than empty words to heal it. The void at the heart of all things will never be filled, and these words are just another attempt to fill it. And nor do we need to empty the void of the attempt to fill the void. The void will remain, whatever we do or don't do to it.

Let the void be.

And the moment you do that, it's over. The whole damn thing. Not only is it over, but it never really happened. See, it's gone. Like a childhood monster that was never there.

*

Night-time voices calling to each other, across and within and through the void which I am not separate from, mixing and meshing and swirling until it all becomes as clear as a punch to the stomach: *There is only the void.*

And I die and become the void. And the void is me and I am the void. I am those voices calling to each other. Separate and whole at the same time. One and many together. This is a this is a not-this is a this in an infinitely regressing spiral of being and non-being, and suddenly it's all dancing, motiveless, purposeless, pointless again. The purpose of the dance is the dance. God himself dances, and it all ends here, where it all began.

Here. Now. This moment. It is all undone.

Dialogues II

Q. There's a feeling of incompleteness that won't go away. Part of me thinks it will go away if I get the right answers to my questions. But then I think that in my continuing to ask these questions, I'm prolonging seeking.

A. It's great that you see that your questions are just part of the seeking game. But that's fine; questions don't ever need to be denied. They may arise, or they may not; you don't really have any choice in the matter!

But asking a question implies that there is an answer, and that you don't have that answer yet. The questioning comes out of the feeling of incompleteness which you talk about. Look at this feeling of incompleteness. The mind says "To get rid of this feeling of incompleteness, I must find answers!" And so can you see how this actually maintains the feeling of incompleteness? In reality, there is no "incompleteness" there; that's just a story, a belief.

As long as there is asking-questions-and-waiting-for-answers, there will be incompleteness. But this feeling of incompleteness arises now. Just feel it. It's just energy in the body. Without labelling it "incompleteness" what does it feel like? Even to so-called "self-realized" people, this feeling may arise from time to time. But it's just a feeling, like any other.

This feeling is fine, seeking is fine, asking questions is fine, waiting for answers is fine. All of it *already* arises in liberation. There is breathing, the beating of the heart, the sounds of footsteps out in the street, the rumble of the traffic outside. This is all there is. *Already* it just happens for no-one, it just arises out of nowhere. It simply *is*. Any question you could ask would imply that there is something *more* than this, that there is some "completeness" beyond this. But there is ONLY this.

And watch the mind as it keeps going "But there must be MORE than this!"

(And that's fine too!)

You say that for "you" it was a gradual thing but surely there must have been a tipping point so to speak, when belief turned to knowing, doubt to certainty?

Well – right now, I have no certainty whatsoever!!

It's the feeling of certainty that was gradually seen through, I think. I used to be so certain about who I was, about what enlightenment was, about what "state" I should aim for. These days, the only thing I know is that I cannot know a damn thing. And actually, I don't even know that.

For there's only ever this – awareness and its passing content. Right now, there is the beat of the heart, breathing, birds singing outside, thoughts coming and going. And that's IT. It's so damn simple and so damn obvious. We're all in liberation all the time and yet we spend our lives searching for something more than what is presently given in this moment.....

And yes, there may be the belief "I just don't get it yet" or "I wish I was more certain" or "I'm not as enlightened as I should be." And these thoughts just float in awareness. It all just *happens*; it all arises for nobody. And all of us already know this. But we search for something else, something more than this. Some "higher" state. These days, that, to me, seems so silly, so funny, because already in our awareness right now is 100% enlightenment, 100% liberation.

Just this is it. Just this. Isn't this the simplest of messages?

And now notice how the mind may object: "But it can't be that simple!"

If you had one tip to give me as to how to proceed – what would it be?

Well, I don't think its a question of doing anything else. Perhaps it's a question of noticing – right here, right now, and in every moment – how the mind wants something more, something else, something more than just this. In this moment it may be waiting for me to give some sort of answer as to how to proceed, and then, not getting an answer, it may move on to the next "source of answers"...

For me, "liberation" (for want of a better word) is just this: breathing, hunger in belly, birds singing outside, thoughts of "I should get some food" or "I need to file that application before tomorrow", pain in left knee....
Just that.... and nothing more.

It's so easy – this is already liberation. But it sure doesn't seem that way!

Ah yes. Perhaps that's because you have an idea of what it *should* seem like!

There are times of great clarity. But the problem is that the imagination comes back in and seeking starts over again.

Ah.... well, it's so simple! Imagination (thought) is supposed to carry on; who said it should ever stop? Perhaps it will stop when you're dead! You see, thought is fine, imagination is fine. It just floats through awareness. There is breathing, the beating of the heart, hunger, pain, noises from outside, the boiling of the kettle, and thoughts floating through. Perhaps the thought "I should be free from thoughts by now, what's wrong with me?", or perhaps the thought "I want to reach an enlightened state that is free from all thoughts of self, all desire, all suffering!" All of that is fine, it does not need to be denied. Denying it would just be more thought. I think there is a tendency for people on certain "spiritual" paths to think that thought is "bad", or thoughts of self shouldn't arise. But isn't that just more thought?

The reality: *thought appears.* It's so simple. It's so obvious. Thought simply appears. What tends to happen is that thoughts of "me" appear, and then, because of all the spiritual books we've read, we think "Oh no, that shouldn't happen anymore, I thought I was becoming more liberated!" But that, too, is just *more* thought.

Nobody has ever ended thought using thought. Which is to say, nobody has ever ended thought at all. Thought arises – let it be.

This message is so simple: liberation is just this. Here. Now. Breathing … sipping tea …. cars rushing outside … a cat pouncing on the tree in the garden... And the thought "I just don't get it!" or "I wish the sense of 'me' would subside!" But those thoughts are fine too. They are just thoughts. Trying to get rid of them is just more thought. Let it all be.

It's so utterly simple, and the mind complicates it, setting goals and aims and telling you you're not "there" yet. We are all already there, because we are all already *here*. Right here. Look around you – can you imagine wanting anything other than this? If you can, can you see how that is just thought (the conditioned mind) telling you that there is something better? And that is the search. But the search is fine... it doesn't need to be denied. Thought *already* arises for no-one. Liberation is *already* 100% here.

There is a tension here I want to get rid of. Once you're a self-realized person....

… ah, there are no self-realized people! It's a contradiction in terms. But if there are, it is every single one of us. Including "you". The search for "self-realization" is the lie we've been falling for our whole lives – the idea that there is some state better than the current state.

There is no self to realize; there are no enlightened individuals. There is only *this*. Of course, what might arise are thoughts of self-realization, of enlightenment, of enlightened individuals, of "ending the search". All these thoughts, and more, float through awareness; and that's fine and wonderful!

And there may be a belief that these thoughts have some reality to them; that there is some "answer" out there, something beyond the thoughts, waiting to be discovered. And this is the merry-go-round that we all seem to be on! Just for one moment, consider the possibility that it *is* just a merry-go-round. Where does that leave us? Here. Now. Breathing. Thoughts floating through. Just this, just this – already this is the liberation that is sought. As long as it's being sought, there is the tension you speak about. The tension is fine too. The seeking is fine. But there is ONLY the tension, only the seeking; there is nothing to be found at the "end" of the search (that idea just maintains the search!); there is nothing to "get".

Perhaps it will be seen, by no-one, that this seeking is in vain, and that there is only ever *this*, what is clearly given in this moment. And you know what? This is *already* seen (no future required!). You're seeing it now (right now!) but you keep denying it because you expect it to feel special, or "spiritual". Ah, that's the secret: *Liberation is ordinary life, just as it is. Nothing – absolutely nothing – needs to be "seen" for this to be.*

The "you" will always arise. Tension will arise. Frustration will arise. Pain will arise. Tears will flow. Desire will come and go. The secret is that all of this is *already* arising for no-one. We're all already living in liberation. It's the idea that something needs to be "seen" before you can "get" this that drives the search. The search already arises for no-one, out of no-thing, here, now, as it is.

Feel frustration now? Feel tension now? Feel confusion now? Just that is liberation.

Ah, did you expect something more than just this?

Did you expect liberation not to include frustration, tension and confusion?

What sort of liberation would that be, if it did not include everything?

What sort of God would that be; a God who did not appear in and as all the things of this world?

Enlightenment (for want of a better word) is the ultimate disappointment, if you're looking for something "special".

What happened to you?

You know, really I don't think anything "happened" to me. If anything, all that happened was this: I (apparently) stopped waiting for something to happen!

It wasn't a sudden thing; there was no flash of light and thunder (that's the illusion!). It was so simple: just a gradual lessening of believing the story "I need something other than this!" That was the "final block", as it were (although of course, there are no blocks!).

I realised that even desiring liberation or enlightenment or awakening is just another desire, just another "block" to the perfection of this moment. But you know, in truth, you can't stop desiring, and you can't stop waiting for that "final block" to fall away – that's still a "doing".

So, just notice when you find a state of waiting occurring, when the thought "This isn't it, I'll be there soon" arises and is believed. Just notice that. Notice how that is the very thing that, in that moment, is blocking you from the joy and utter simplicity of this moment.

It's very very subtle, but when you notice what you're apparently doing to yourself you may start to laugh! And then you may find yourself looking around at all the things in the room, and listening to all the sounds – the cat miaowing (if you have one!), the kettle boiling, your heart beating – and realising that this is IT! There is nothing more than *this*, more than *now*. Look around – isn't it a gift?!

It all comes down to living each moment as if it's your last. The search for liberation implies a future, so it's an illusion. This may be your last moment on Earth. If it is, why would you ignore it by placing your hope in some future liberation? *Now* is all there is. Stop, now, and notice. And now. And now......

Are you "awake"?

I'm only as "awake" as you are! The only thing that has changed is that these days the dream of individuality has lost its hold. Often the same thoughts that used to plague me still arise, but these days I simply don't place any importance on them. They simply float through awareness. It's amazing what happens when thought is seen for what it is.

There's no effort in it. No choice. They are just thoughts. They aren't personal.

Striving for an "awakened" state is just another habitual thought pattern. "I am not awake yet" or "I am not awake enough yet": these very thoughts are the ones "clouding" your awakened state, which is already 100% present (and yet, liberation can never really be "clouded" at all…).

See what happens. In the play of life, the thought "I need to be awake" arises, and that thought is attached to, it is given importance. And then you (the individual) feel like a failure, right? You feel like you're missing out? Here's the secret: the problem is not that you're "not awake yet". The problem (and it's not really a problem at all) is that there is the belief that "I need to be awake" or "I should be awake now, but I'm not". See how that belief gives the individual the illusion that there is something to achieve, that this moment isn't enough. See how it clouds the perfection of this moment. See how it actually apparently clouds this already awakened state!

"I'm a failure – I'm not awake yet like those enlightened guys I've read about." Without that thought, without that striving for this "state of perfection" or "state of pure joy" or whatever image arises, without all of that stress, how would you live? It would be a huge relief, wouldn't it?

It's the *search* for enlightenment that is the apparent problem. Enlightenment, if it is anything, is the end to the search for enlightenment! And yet, you cannot think yourself out of this paradox. You cannot tell yourself "I must stop the search". This is the part I apparently struggled with for ages! I was kicking myself all the time because I didn't believe I was in that state I read and read about. It sounded so good! A state free from suffering and desire! I read all the stuff you read, and it made me feel, well, inferior! But you see, the desire for enlightenment, or permanent awakening, is just another desire, but perhaps the most subtle of all, and the hardest to spot, and you can probably feel that desire right now. When the individual believes "I'm not awakened yet, and I should be by now", the individual will undoubtedly feel frustration.

Really, all that crap, that bullshit, about enlightenment has to leave your system. You have to give up, totally give up! And yet, "you" cannot give up! As the Buddha said, "I achieved absolutely nothing from pure, unexcelled enlightenment." And J. Krishnamurti meant the same thing when he said "Truth is a pathless land". That means truth is NOW. Truth is this moment. Truth is THIS. Truth IS.

It cannot be denied, it cannot be avoided. It simply is. How can we deny "is"?

But the mind hears that and goes "Well, that's very nice". And then carries on searching! Just watch the mind as it throws up thoughts like "If I carry on with my practice, I'll be enlightened" or "What's wrong with me, I'm not as awake as these guys I'm reading about!". But as "these guys" say over and over, you are already that which you seek! So stop seeking! (The problem is the mind hears that and feels deflated! "What do you mean stop seeking? There must be something better than this!")

Seeking is the problem, and yet "you" cannot stop seeking. Can you see why an individual may be on this merry-go-round for an entire lifetime?

Can we get back to basics? Tell me again, what is liberation?

It's so simple. Sitting on a chair, the sound of the heart beating, breathing, the miaowing of my cat, voices chattering. Just that, as it is.

And the mind goes "There must be more than this", or "You need to awaken, then you'll enjoy this more!" Before, I used to take all that seriously and feel crap about it. "I want enlightenment! I want what the spiritual teachers have!" But that was just another desire!! These days, I (apparently) let those thoughts float by. They are just thoughts!! If I believed them, they would take me away from this moment. I would miss *this*.

So come back to this moment. Come back to your breathing. The sensations in the body. Awareness, and the contents of awareness (and these are not-two). That is all there is. The endless search for enlightenment would take you away from this. It would be a denial of the very reality that stares you in the face at this moment.

As Zen says, enlightenment is "nothing special". It's just this. This moment. Breathing. A chair over there, a mug over there, a table. Thoughts floating through. Perhaps some apparent attachment to those thoughts. Perhaps thoughts about awakening, or worries about the future. Or regrets over the past. But let them float through. Can you see you already are perfect? You breathe right on cue. Your heart beats perfectly in time. Thoughts arise and fall away.

The ordinary mind is always already enlightened; we just think it's not, and so we search for enlightenment in the future and it drives us crazy. And we ignore the reality in front of us. Ignoring reality can never be a good thing. After all, it's reality!

What I'm really trying to say is that you are always *already* free. See through the search, see it for the lie that it is. The lie that promises us that there is something more than this.

Which is to say, notice those thoughts that take you away from this, that project into some imagined future and say "I'll be happy *then*, I'll be perfect *then*."

There is never a "then". "Then" always arises now. There is only ever now. If you cannot be happy now, you will never be happy. And yet, everything you do to try and become happy is the very feeling of unhappiness that you want to be rid of! Seeing through this craziness is the ending of it. And yet it's not something "you" can do.

I wish I'd never heard of this enlightenment stuff. It's driving me mad. I'll need another 300 years to awaken!

Yes, you have a point. It *is* a curse! It's all conceptual, second-hand information passed down to you. It all has to leave your system. Come back to you. Come back to this moment. Reject everything anyone has ever told you. *It all could be false.* Go on your own present evidence. Come back to your own awareness now. The awareness of things in the room. Your breathing.

And the thought "I'll need another 300 years to awaken". Can you see it as just a thought, arising in awareness now? Can you see how, if you believe that thought, it makes you feel like crap? Feel the sensations it gives you. Can you see it's just a thought, a pile of mental images? An image of yourself in a "perfect" state sometime in the future? Can you see how that image is the problem? There's no problem outside of that image, the image of a future perfection. Just allow that image to be there.

"If you see the Buddha, kill him" is a Zen saying. That is, the image of the Buddha, the image of enlightenment, the image of perfection is the very thing that keeps you on the search. But notice: that mind-created ideal just appears in awareness. It's not personal. It's like a cloud floating by. It will stay for a bit, and pass, as all things do.

That image arises now. But it tricks you, it claims that there is a future in which you could be happier, more enlightened, more liberated. But where does the future exist, apart from as thought, arising now?

Is there really any such thing as the future? Is there really any such thing as the past? Or is there only ever the eternal present, in which "past" thoughts and "future" thoughts arise?

Will this not also be the case five seconds from now? Five years from now? Is there ever a time when it is not *now*? Is there ever a time when the past and future do not arise merely as thought? Doesn't this completely destroy the fantasy of "becoming liberated at some point in the future"?

I try to observe thoughts, but I can't seem to do it. I feel a deep despair.

It sounds like you are observing thoughts in order to get somewhere, you are doing it with a motive. Can you see that? Very subtly, you think that if you observe thoughts "well enough", eventually you may become enlightened like those guys you've read about.

Can you see how you are looking for happiness in a future time?

But, as the Buddha said, there is no way to happiness – happiness *is* the way. And that may sound very far-out, but it really points to the simplest of things: that the only block to happiness is the search for happiness. See through the search. Come back to this moment. Present awareness. Breathing. Your own world. Your own experience, not those experiences you've read about. The sights and smells and sounds of the room you're in. That is all there is. That is "what is". It is heaven.

And then the thought *"This isn't good enough! I want to awaken! I can't believe it hasn't happened to me yet"!* And that is HELL!

Here's a nice little quote that pretty much says it all:

"The search ends with the realization that there is no such thing as enlightenment. By searching, you want to be free from the self, but whatever you are doing to free yourself from the self is the self. How can I make you understand this simple thing? There is no 'how'. If I tell you that, it will only add more momentum to the search...."

– U.G. Krishnamurti.

It sounds like you're saying that everything is perfect. Well, over here, everything is certainly not perfect! What's it like for you?

The word "perfection" is, like all words, dead the moment it is spoken, whilst reality, *this*, is alive, alive, alive, ever changing, always moving, always fresh, always exciting! Maybe that is what is really meant by "perfection"; the perfection of the whole damn mess, as it is; a perfection which actually *embraces* all imperfection. It wouldn't really be a very good perfection if it didn't, would it?

What I do find these days is that everything is now so *interesting*; pain is interesting, grief is interesting, genocide is interesting, corporations are interesting, the situation in Iraq is interesting, my crazy work colleague yelling at me is interesting; whereas before it was all so serious, so very serious. Life has taken on the quality of a dream, a game, a show. And it always *was* that, I'd just apparently forgotten.

This isn't a cold detachment. I'd still perhaps cheer for a war protester, or cry over a sentimental novel, or laugh at a stupid teenage comedy film; it's just that none of it goes that *deep* anymore. Even intense pain somehow has a huge spaciousness around it. I simply cannot *convince* myself of anything. And the past feels so unreal...

I don't know; words just pale in comparison; words don't capture it at all. Words just float in this awareness. They complement the sound of the coffee maker, the cat miaowing, the radio buzzing......

It used to be my wish that everyone in the world could see this. But isn't that just another want, another desire, another part of the search? People absolutely do not need to "get this", not at all. Not in the slightest. Not that there's anything to "get"...

Oh – such paradoxes when you try to say it!

I've been trying to end thought for years. But even if my thoughts weren't there for a while they'd come back eventually. Being in a painful decaying body is a problem. This world is a problem. I'm not cut out for this!

Upon "realisation" (for want of a better word!) thoughts do not end. This is the major "mistake" that people apparently make. Thoughts continue, but perhaps it is seen: thoughts are not personal. They just arise and dissolve in awareness. Like clouds drifting through the sky.

The mistake people make is to TRY and end thought. But this is always doomed to failure and frustration, because the attempt to end thought is just more thinking. If we try to end thought, we're just adding more layers of thought. We're trying to end thought using thought. Hopeless!

The reason I say you are already free, you are already liberated, is that already thought is not personal; already the self is an illusion, in the sense that it is just another appearance in awareness.

If you are already That which you seek, then why does it feel like you're not? Because you are still seeking! This was, for example, Ramana Maharshi's ultimate message. However, to those people who "didn't quite get it", he also taught to seek the root of the "I". Ultimately, it would be seen to be an illusion, and therefore all seeking for it would fall away. It's the paradox. You are already that which you seek, you are Awareness itself, you are Spirit, but you believe that you're not, and so you seek for It in the future. But what you Are must be present right now, in this moment. Who you Are must be 100% present right now. That is why seeking it in the future is the very thing that prevents you seeing it now. The seeking IS the very ego that you want to be rid of.

Can you see that it is only an ego that would seek for enlightenment as a future event? It is an ego that desires to be free of ego. THAT is the paradox...

And there is nobody who is "not cut out for this". That's not even possible.

This message sounds very complex, very heady...

Well, really it is the simplest of all messages. *This is all there is.* But the mind interprets and says "I must do something to *get* that". No – anything you do is just adding more thought. Simply notice the movement of thought, pulling you into a future moment where you will be "enlightened". Come back to the present moment. Who is the one who wants enlightenment? That ego must be present now. That ego IS thought. Who is aware of thought, who is aware of the little individual self?

When you "get" it (and you already have, you're just not admitting it!) it will feel so obvious. So natural. So ordinary that the mind will go "This can't be it!" You will kick yourself for seeking something spectacular all these years. It's this feeling of "This can't be it!" that blocks it. Because this, now, is it! Enlightenment does not come in a flash of neon light and exploding fireworks. It is simple, obvious, utterly ordinary. It is the ending of all seeking.

But it is not something to achieve. It is something that *already* has been achieved; it is something that already is. There's nothing you can do – or not do – to get it.

So no more seeking is needed. You are already enlightened. The Answer of all Answers must be present right now, in this moment. You don't need the future to be who you are, or to become what you are.

Aaagh! My head hurts! Too many paradoxes! I kind of get it though. I sometimes feel peaceful for a while, but then the madness is back! Any suggestions? I've spent way too much money on books!

Well yes, this seeking malarkey can get very expensive! I too spent hundreds of pounds on books. I always hoped that *"This book will be the last one! This will be the book that 'does it' for me!"*

Of course, it's a nice dream. You could spend your whole life waiting for this to "click". But of course, is there anything to "click"? Or is that just a hope? Is that just an escape from THIS, from this present life, this present appearance?

You see, as long as you're trying to escape the present, as long as you're trying to "get" to a future time when you'll be liberated, or enlightened, or just "get it at last", you're on the search! And the search to "put an end to the search" is just part of the search!

The frustration you feel is perhaps because you're starting to realise this; that it's a futile effort, a futile escape from what is. What is, is already fully present. Present sights, smells, thoughts.

Notice when you are trying to escape to a future time when you'll "get it". That is the only frustration. When that is seen through, THIS becomes very exciting! Why would we want anything else?

You say you feel peaceful sometimes, but then "the madness is back". You're implying that you want the peace, but not the madness. But when the "madness" is happening, that is what is. That is the texture of the moment. You project a future moment when you'll be "peaceful". And that is more of the search.

This future "peaceful state" is just an idea, a belief, an image based on all the images from those books that you've read, probably! Come back to now. This is all there is. The future is just a thought. If there is madness, that is fine. If there is pain, that is fine. All arises in the being that you are. Being is never tainted by what happens. It simply doesn't matter what arises. The more you fight what arises, the more frustration there will be.

If the "madness" is not seen as madness, is it madness?

Madness and peace – one and the same. All equal, all permissible. All arise in THIS, all arise now. Everything ALREADY arises for nobody, it ALREADY arises in this open space. There is room for everything.

Liberation is already *this*. But as long as you're searching for it in the future, there will be trouble.

But the search does not need to be given up. The search is fine. It may be seen through, or not. Either way, that is liberation.

When all is said and done: what is wrong with THIS moment?

So, what you're really saying is that once we stop caring about the present moment...that is liberation?

Well, there may be the story "When I truly don't care about what is happening now, there will be liberation".

But whoever said liberation is "not caring about what happens"? That's just another story, another belief, another idea … all of which apparently obscures the ever-present liberation (although of course, it can never really be obscured – for it is THIS, here now).

See how the tricky little mind keeps on churning out those stories about "what liberation will be like, when it finally happens"?

Can all these stories be seen (by no-one) as JUST that – stories arising now?

The story of liberation, of enlightenment, of awakening – it's JUST another story, arising now. And when that story is believed, this ever-present liberation is apparently ignored.

This, right here, right now, is heaven. And heaven includes it all: self, pain, pleasure, thoughts, beliefs, desires, longing to be free...

We've been expecting something more our whole lives! Could it be that there is nothing more? Just the belief that there is "something more"?

Liberation, if it is anything, is the seeing-through of the hope for a *future* happiness, a *future* salvation, a *future* enlightenment. But nothing is "gained" by this seeing-through. If anything, everything is (apparently) lost! This is certainly not an achievement – nothing to be aimed for. Nothing that "you" would really want!

Liberation is ordinary life as it already is: going to the toilet, getting cancer, experiencing excruciating pain, losing loved ones, earning money, paying the bills, growing old, losing your sight, pissing yourself at night...

Did we ever expect anything more?

Our longing to be free from this life and all its apparent problems is exactly what keeps us bound to it.

Right. I've talked long enough. Time for *X-Factor*...

PART THREE

Life Without a Centre

"You don't need to leave your room. Remain sitting at your table and listen. Don't even listen, simply wait. Don't even wait, be quite still and solitary. The world will freely offer itself to you to be unmasked. It has no choice. It will roll in ecstasy at your feet."

– Franz Kafka

The Miracle

To see without the seer, without the delusion – that's the miracle.

But even to speak of the miracle, even that is part of the delusion. For the speaking of the miracle implies a speaker and that which is spoken of – the very duality which the miracle is the ending of. But to say that the duality may be "ended" implies a path to its ending. No, there is no ending to delusion; even the idea of a path towards the ending of delusion is part of the delusion. There is no path, there is no ending of delusion, for the delusion never began, which is to say that the miracle never ended. The miracle is present, now, in this moment, if you would only stop looking for it, if you would only stop looking for an end to delusion.

The very idea of delusion is delusion, the idea of the ending of delusion is delusion. What is not delusion?

*

Ah, words will never capture it, as words themselves spring from the delusional state of consciousness that is taken as normality. That which is beyond the words will never be spoken of, and it will never be known, for both the speaker and the knower already are part of the delusion. Nor can the reality behind the words be experienced, for there is no experiencer.

No seer, no knower, no speaker, no experiencer. Only this, this moment, without beginning or end. So we cannot even really speak of this moment; for that implies division: this moment divided from the next moment, this moment as a slither of time between the past and present. No, the moment we speak of this moment we speak in untruths, for in reality there is no moment separate from the next moment, that is to say, there is no time altogether. Nor is there the timeless, for the timeless can only be known in relation to time.

So what is there? You will never know. Anything you can know is not what you seek. The knowing is the problem; the seeking is the problem. What happens when all that just drops away? What is revealed? Can there be a willingness to find out? Can there be a plunge into the unknown?

Perhaps there can be, if you are fearless enough. There can be total loss of self, of identity, of knowledge; which is not to say that these things simply disappear, rather they are seen to be illusory, the source of all misery. They then lose their fearful grip on you. However, you can still use them, but you are not ruled by them. And then suffering is seen for what it truly is: a dream, no more, no less.

But that is a statement about what the dropping of these things is NOT; what the dropping of these things IS you will never know conceptually, which is to say you will never know at all. You have to take the plunge to find out. And yet, "you", the primary illusion in all of this, cannot take the plunge, for "you" are a creation of thought.

But perhaps the plunge will be taken, by nobody, without cause, without intent, without purpose. Perhaps, then, there will just be the simplicity of what is, with nobody there to interpret, to create meaning, to evaluate; and yet there will still be the light streaming through the window, a squirrel burying his stash of food, the sound of breathing, the wind shaking the leaves from the trees ... but now unconditional love will be the ground from which all things arise, and the ground back to which all things eventually return....

Perhaps that is possible. I really don't know. Nor do I give a damn anymore.

Perfection in Imperfection

There is no security in this life, none whatsoever. There is nothing to which we can cling. All things will fade away in time. Those whom we love will die. That which we hold fast to now will dissolve, will crumble to the ground, will turn to ash and dust.

There is only the illusion of security, which is maintained by our constant seeking for an end to our imagined insecurity. Beyond security and insecurity, there is freedom, but this freedom will never be found through seeking...

*

See through the illusory nature of this thing you call life. It is nothing more than a dream, a play of consciousness. It is without purpose or meaning. There is neither origin nor destination, nowhere to go and nobody to go there. There is only ever Now. And the only suffering is the illusion of past and future. Seeing through this convincing illusion is liberation... but the grand cosmic joke is that you are always already liberated, and once more, there is no "you" to be liberated in the first place.

But beyond this paradox of language, beyond all dualistic notions of good and evil, self and no-self, beginning and end, light and dark, God and the devil, Heaven and Hell – beyond all mind-created duality, there is Consciousness in all its purity, and you are That. Reading these words. Trying to make sense of them. Being utterly confused, or not. Just that, as it is, is liberation.

You see, all sentient beings are always already liberated, always already free, though apparently many believe they are not! And that, too, is fine. It's all perfect the way it is. Wars, genocides, famines, illness, hunger, violence, pain, suffering: how could it be any other way?

There is perfection in imperfection. Indeed, that is the only perfection there is.

God in All Things

"So waiting, I have won from you the end:
God's presence in each element."

– Goethe

There is a powerful stillness out of which all things arise, and people have termed this stillness God, or the Tao, or the Buddha Mind, or Allah, or the Christ Within; but the stillness is not any of these things. Rather, it is pointed at by these things, but transcends, and includes, all of them.

But it seems we are terrified of this stillness, and we tiptoe around it for most of our lives. Stillness is the void which consumes everything, all identity, all past and future, all hope and fear and pleasure and pain. We are simply terrified to lose our humanity and sink into this divinity, but therein lies our salvation: to die, literally, into God. Which is death into all things: for all things are God.

The trees, the birds, the road, the cars, the people going about their daily business, all that is God. The suffering in the faces of these people; that too, is God. The smiles as they greet each other, the tears as loved ones part, the anger and the violence and the fear and the longing to be free from it all; all that, too, is God. There is nothing, literally nothing, that is not God.

And so to split God up into various religions and

doctrines and ideologies, to shrink Him into belief-sized chunks; that is nothing but idolatry, and the real lie is that it is not seen as idolatry, but "the way to God". Any way to God implies that God is not already here, now, and that is a denial of the God that stares you in the face at this moment. Look around you. Is this not God? If not, where is He to be found? When will you find Him?

*

The search for God is in vain, for He stands in front of you now, in and as all the things of this world. Hold out your hand: there is the hand of God. Look down at your legs: the legs of the divine. The bird landing on that branch over there: are you seriously telling me that this is not a manifestation of God?

Look! Look around you! God is in all things! A God that is not in all things is a small God, a God of the mind, a God that requires belief, religion, thought. Is that not idolatry? Is that not a mind-made, man-made idol?

So drop it all! Drop your religions, and come back to this moment, and stare at the very God you've been searching for your whole life. Coming back to Now is real worship, is real prayer, is real meditation, is real faith, for it is only Now that God can be seen, felt, heard, experienced. Feel your breath? Is it not God who breathes through you? Feel your heart beating inside your chest? Is that not the work of God? Do you really need a future to find Him? Is He not with you right now? Is He not literally staring you in the face?

And we'll let Saint Augustine have the final word:

"God is more intimate to me than I am to myself."

A Cup of Tea

"Our life is frittered away by detail . . .
Simplify, simplify!"

– Thoreau.

Perhaps the inexpressible will never be expressed. I don't know. Today, there is only life being played out on the screen of awareness, and nobody in control. It happens spontaneously, which is to say nothing "happens" at all: there is only this, undivided, unfragmented, perfectly itself, arising spontaneously, leaving no trace.

I drink a cup of tea. And yet there is no "I" doing this. "I" is merely a figure of speech, a convenient sound that might be used to confirm that it is indeed this bodymind, rather than any other, which apparently drinks the tea. The hand goes out, the cup comes up, the liquid goes into the mouth and down the throat and into the stomach, and I, if I am anything, am the silent observer behind all of this, the space in which it all appears. And there is no meaning and no purpose behind this play; it happens spontaneously, of its own accord. And the thought "I'm drinking a cup of tea" is all part of this wonderful show.

No, I do not drink the tea, for there is no tea and no "I" who can drink, and certainly no "I" separate from any drinkable tea. There is only the tea, only the cup, only the liquid rushing through the body, but nobody here to claim this as a self-initiated action.

But still, I drink a cup of tea! It's simpler just to say that, and be done with it. *I do not drink a cup of tea, but apparently I do.*

Still, it's a nice cup of tea.

Perhaps drinking tea can save the world. When there is drinking of tea with no desire to do anything *other* than drink tea ("when drinking, just drink"), all violence, division, anxiety and fear dissolve; because there is *only* the moment, *only* the drinking of the tea, and in the moment suffering is always just a projection, a belief, based on memory. Come back to the tea, and where is the past? Where is the future? Where is the rest of the world? Where are your enemies?

Perhaps this will save the world: people coming back to the simple things, and finding the joy inherent in them.

Or perhaps it is too late. Either way, it doesn't really matter. Enjoy this world while it lasts. And more importantly, enjoy this moment while it lasts.

Or not!

No World

The primary delusion of human consciousness: "I am a person, in the world."

I am not in the world. Rather, the world is in me. But to say "The world is in me" implies that there may be things, events, places outside of me. No, *all* things are in me. There is nothing, no thing, outside. And so no inside either, because outside can only be known in reference to inside.

And so there is no me (because I have no inside and no outside), and no things. Only *this*. There was never any separation in the first place. There was never any "me" separate from all things. That was the illusion.

*

Everything that is arising is seen, but by no-one. I do not see all that arises: I am all that arises; all that arises sees itself.

*

Try and speak of it, and we immediately fall into error, because to speak of it implies that there is somebody here to speak of it. Which implies an "it" and somebody separate from "it". But there is only "it", and no "I" separate from "it".

So there are only these words, which write themselves. It all happens spontaneously, without intention or purpose. These words appear. And perhaps the thought "I am writing". But that's just a thought. In reality, there is only the tap-tap-tap on the keyboard, and words appearing, which seem to form coherent (!) structures. But there is no sense of doing, no sense of ownership, no sense that these words "belong to me", or that I really have done anything here at all. Tap-tap-tap. The flash of letters appearing on the screen. No, I do not do this. It is done. And there is no "I" separate from all of this.

The "I" is a construction of thought appearing in this moment. But this moment does not require self-conscious constructions of thought. This moment requires nothing; nothing except presence. And there is no way presence can be lost. Sure, it can be "clouded" somewhat by the conceptual overlay of the "I" (the human condition), but never, ever lost. And never found, for how can you find something that you've never lost?

*

Presence, awareness, this moment. That is all there is. Nothing outside of it. And if there was, who would know it? Me? A conceptual overlay from the past; a conceptual overlay that IS the past? Can the past touch the present? Can the past touch this moment? Can these words, which attempt to point to this moment, even come close to this moment? Can anything touch this moment?

*

Anything said about this moment is never said about *this* moment, for this moment is already gone the moment it is spoken of, and it is already a new moment… and a new moment… and a new moment…. bringing new delights, new wonders, new experiences, new sights and sounds and smells…..

This moment will never be captured in words. That said, don't we spend our lives trying to capture this moment in words? Don't philosophers and scientists and metaphysicians and theologians spend their lives trying to "understand" Ultimate Reality – which is this moment?

Ah, the madness of the human mind. In its attempt to "understand", it creates the very confusion it is trying to overcome. In its thirst for knowledge, it creates igno-rance. In its quest for truth, it speaks only in untruths. In its longing for peace, it goes to war.

So let it all drop. Be still. Forget the world and come to know your own mind, the conceptual filter through which the apparent world is apparently experienced. And come to see that there is no world outside of your own mind. The mind is the world, and the world is the mind. And come to experience the freedom and release in dropping everything you think, everything you claim to know. Taste the liberation in the realisa-tion that you don't know a damn thing, that you can't know a damn thing, not about this moment, anyway, and that you never were a little subject in a world full of nasty objects, but you are the presence, the aware-ness, the consciousness that allows the apparent world with its apparent things to be in the first place. And that presence, awareness, consciousness is not separate from all those apparent things! *The world is you, and you are the world.* Did you ever think otherwise? Did you really believe you were a self, an ego, an individual cut off from the whole, a little person in a sea of other people? Well, it was a nice illusion.....

And now you may find that the world drops away, mind drops away, to reveal only this, which has been here all along. And what an astonishing and mysterious thing this – this moment – is.

And it's gone before you can even think about it!

The Last Day

When the Zen master Fa-ch'ang was dying, a squirrel
screeched up on the roof.
"It's just this," Fa-ch'ang said, "and nothing more."

– Zen story.

Truly, every day feels like the last day of my life.

When it is not merely understood intellectually, but seen, as a reality, that past and future are only real in the sense that they are constructions of the mind – in other words mental objects that arise in consciousness in the present moment, and not any other moment (as if there could be any other moment!) – then life takes on a whole new dimension. Life, living, becomes primary, that is, the living moment is seen to be everything, with nothing outside of it.

You no longer live in the past or future, as it were, but you come right back to the place that you never really left, the place where everything happens, the place that is your true home. And everything feels new, fresh, alive, spontaneous, ever changing, ever evolving.

And because the present moment is always new, what is gone is gone for ever, with each and every passing moment. It becomes memory, a phantom, only real in the sense that the mind is real, but unreal from the perspective of the present moment itself, which requires total action, and not self-conscious thought.

So there is complete attention to whatever one is doing, total action, absolute involvement. This is the end of suffering, because it is the end of a past. And so each moment feels like the first and last moment of your life, each day the first and last day.

It is, to the conditioned mind, a strange thing, but to the awareness that I am in my essence, it is freedom itself. It is the thing that everyone searches for but never finds. It is enlightenment, it is liberation. And you have it already, you just haven't noticed. Indeed, you *are* it!

When the existence of the separate individual is seen through, every day is the last day of your life. In the very best sense!

Death

"Death is not an event in life: we do not live to experience death. If we take eternity to mean not infinite temporal duration but timelessness, then eternal life belongs to those who live in the present."

– Wittgenstein

And so the ultimate secret of our apparent existence is perhaps this: *death is liberation*. It is liberation from the forms of this world, from all suffering, mental and physical, from all problems, from hopes, dreams, desires, ambitions, goals, memories, feelings, from the whole human condition. Which begs the question, perhaps the ultimate question: why do we fear it?

And this begs perhaps the ultimate, ultimate question: who, or what, dies?

It looks like this: "I am afraid that I will be no more. I am afraid of not existing. I am afraid of nothingness, afraid of the unknown." But here's the catch: even the unknown is known. The moment I think of the unknown, the "unknown" is an object of knowledge, an abstraction, an image in the mind, and hence, of course, it is known. Beyond knowledge and ignorance, what is truly Unknown will never be captured by the mind....

So what do I really fear when thinking about my own demise? It is simply this: the end of "me". The end of self. The end of "I". The end of my life story, my saga, my epic, my journey.

But if you look deeply, you will see that "I" is not separate from the entire structure of thought, the entire experiencing structure with which the apparent world is perceived. All of which is to say, when the "I" goes, the whole world goes with it. There is no world apart from my experience of it, in my experience! Perhaps that sounds obvious. But if this is really taken on board, then it is clearly seen that death is not the end. It is merely the end of the personal experiencing structure you take to be yourself. It is the end of the personal, the end of the known, and a plunge into Nothingness.

But answer me this: in what or in whom does this entire experiencing structure arise? That is, put more simply, who is aware of "me", and who is aware that this "me" may end?

Will you be present at your own death? Who will you be at the moment of your death?

For that matter, who were you at the moment of your apparent birth? And a moment before that? Did you simply spring into existence at a specific moment in time, so many years ago? Will you simply spring out of existence at a specific moment in time, so many years from now?

This is the dream. The dream that you were born, and will die.

The end of this dream, the plunge into the Nothingness

that you are, is liberation. And liberation can happen now, in this moment, if you would only drop your entire belief system, your religions, your superstitions, your concepts, everything you have taken on authority. If you would only drop everything you take to be true, you would see truth, not the word, but the experience.

But of course, you cannot drop any anything. The more you try to drop your beliefs, the more they stick.

But perhaps, these things will be seen through, by no-one. And then, truth reveals itself, the truth that was there all along, the truth that is *always* there, all along.

And truth looks like this:

Breathing.....

....a cough.....

.... a bird landing on an electricity pylon over there....

... the wind blowing.....

... the sound of children playing in the garden...

... the thud of my heart beating...

... a dull ache in the left arm...

... the warm mug in my hand...

... a thought popping up about the football match tonight...

....the buzz of the television...

In this moment, right now, where is death? It is nowhere, is it? It's a mental projection, a projection that creates the illusion of future, isn't it?

Is there really anything there apart from images in your mind, feelings in your body?

Isn't it these images, these feelings that you're afraid of?

*

Until death happens, it is always a projection. And the moment death happens, projection ends, fear ends. Death is the end of fear, the end of self, the end of a future.

And so death, or fear of death, is really the grand cosmic joke. The one thing we truly fear is the one thing which, when deeply looked into, will ultimately liberate us, liberate us from itself! Death liberates you from death! And there is really no "you" to be liberated!

So let people die! Let them! They die when they die, and you can't stop it. Yes, you can probably help them to ease their pain somewhat, and that may be the kindest thing to do in the circumstances, but ultimately you won't stop them from dying, which is what you really desire. You must let go of them. Say goodbye now, for you will not save them! And keeping them alive, as if that were possible, will not save you.

*

And of course, you won't stop yourself from dying. You could try, yes, but you'd be fighting a battle you'd ultimately lose. You'd be running in circles your whole life, for the fight against death, the fight against the end of the self, is nothing other than the striving of the self to prevent its own destruction, a striving which IS the self.

Like a dog chasing its own tail...

*

Immortality is the ultimate dream of the ego, the ultimate hope, and the ultimate madness. But it seems we're all locked in the madness. We all want to be immortal. Or at least, we all want to live. Or at least, we don't want to die! Not yet, anyway. Hopeless! Madness! You WILL die! You will die in spite of your efforts to live! You may die tomorrow!

*

Yes, you may die tomorrow. So why are you spending today suffering, believing in your non-existent problems? Go, live! Live totally! Live joyously! Live without fear! Live as though you had nothing to defend! Drop your beliefs, drop your ideologies, drop your prejudices, drop every form of suffering and live! Do it now, you may as well – it will be done for you anyway the moment the body stops functioning! Why wait until then? The time is now – there is no other time!

*

To stare death in the face, and fall on the floor laughing
– that is enlightenment.

On Love and Aloneness

I am alone in the garden. The sun is rising. A little robin tugs at a worm in the grass.

In true love, there is no object of desire, affection and tenderness; for the object of desire, affection and tenderness, the beloved, has collapsed into the lover. The object has collapsed into the subject, and there is only love: only love, and nobody to be aware of it; nobody to know it and nobody to deny it. Only love, both radically alone, and intimately connected to all things...

For a subject and an object can never be in love; they are forever divided from each other, split from each other; they can only gaze longingly into each other's eye across an unbridgeable divide, with the fervent hope that one day, one day, love will bridge the chasm, and the isolation of multiplicity and fragmentation will give way to the joy of intimate companionship, togetherness, unity. But no, love cannot and will not bridge the gap, for the gap is inherent in the subject-object split; indeed, the gap *is* the subject-object split, and nothing can fill a gap which is so deeply and fundamentally engrained into the very foundations of our experience. No, love cannot bridge the gap, because a subject and object, a lover and the beloved, are inherently, fundamentally separate. It is unlikely they will ever truly meet as people, as human beings.

But true love is the death of this terrible divide, and

with it, the ending of all division between two people. But this will never be achieved through effort. The very effort to end the division strengthens the division, gives power to the division. For the division is not there. It has never been there, and it will never be there. The division is an illusion, and when you fight an illusion you must always lose.

Lovers will never meet through effort, though they may die trying.

*

So, our lovers continue to gaze longingly at each other across this unbridgeable divide, a divide that they unwittingly have created for themselves. How to help them? Any effort they would make to come together will pull them more strongly apart. Are they doomed to live and die like this? Is there a way out?

There is, but it involves death. Not physical death, but death of the ego; death of everything that separates, death of everything that fragments, death of everything that divides, death of everything that isolates, death of everything that has been carried over from the past, death of everything that projects into the future. Death of the idea of love itself. And finally, finally, it will involve death of the beloved, death of the lover. Death of you and me, and with it, death of all that comes between us. A descent into pure nothingness, a plunge into the unknown.

A risk.

And he who risks in this way may taste it; the sweet and simple joy of radical aloneness that is true love. Look! The robin tweet-tweets as he hops over dew-stained grass, as the morning sun begins to warm and wake the slumbering creatures in this Garden of Eden we have named Earth, and nowhere can I find isolation, loneliness, separation; but all things are in all things, and everywhere is mother, everywhere is home.

And I smile to myself with the realisation of the utterly, utterly obvious: I have not found you, but I have recognised something that has eluded me for a lifetime: *You are not out there, but in here. You are part of the experiencing structure I take to be myself.* And so I do not love you, for there is no "me" to love and no "you" to be loved. No, I do not love you; for you are part of that which loves…

*

And so the great search ends here, now, in this moment. There is only love, and you are that, you are love itself; you are what I feel now, you are the thoughts bubbling up from nowhere and dissolving into nothingness, you are that robin over there, and the fresh dew on the morning grass, and the sun in all its radiance, and we are eternally, timelessly bound in this way, you and me, together with all things, although really there is no "me", no "you", and no things. And we will never be apart, no, we cannot be apart, not now, not ever…

So, this morning, I am alone in the garden, and you are here with me to see it all.

The Tree of Knowledge

"But you must not eat from the tree of the knowledge of good and evil, for when you eat of it you will surely die."
– Genesis 2:17

Truly, we live in our minds.

Out of purest emptiness the entire manifest world arises. Mind is nothing but ripples on the surface of this infinite ocean of emptiness, this vast landscape of silence.

The cosmic dance of colour, form, and motion plays out in this vast spaciousness that I cannot separate myself from, or find myself in. In this emptiness, in this nothingness without beginning or end, there is only this, only what is, and nothing more. Only this, and no eyes to see it, no ears to hear it, no tongue to taste it, no nose to smell it. Eyes would blind it, ears would deafen it, a tongue would render it tasteless.

And when the mind stops its incessant chattering you can sense it, this raging silence, this volcanic peace out of which all things arise, and to which all things return.

But to think of it is to lose it, for it can never be an object of knowledge, it can never be captured by thought.

*

Throughout the ages, men have sought the eternal silence beneath the ripples of life. But they have never attained it, because it is in the very seeking for it that we lose any hope of finding it. It cannot be found, for it is that which is prior to the search – prior to thought, prior to knowledge, prior to rationality. It is that which you see before you. It is this moment. It is now.

And when you think about it, it's already gone, it's already a new moment, and your search prevented the seeing of it. A moment captured by thought is already an old moment, it is already dead. You killed it yourself.

*

And yet there are no old moments, no dead moments, only the eternal present. Think about the past, and the thoughts appear in this moment. Think about the future, and those thoughts appear in this moment too. All thought appears now, now, and now.... and yet we still fall for the illusion of past and future as concrete realities. But nobody has ever touched the past, except in present thoughts. And nobody has ever touched the future, except in present thoughts. Past and future are illusions, nothing more. And they happen now, now and now. Even these words are being interpreted through the filter of the past, through memory. How else would you understand?

But look! A plane rumbles faintly overhead, a bird chirps away on the branches of that tree, somebody coughs, flowers sway gently in the breeze – and where in any of this can you find a past? Where in any of this can you find a future?

*

Past is memory. Future is projection based on memory. And yet they both drive us insane. Because with past and future come a sense of self, a sense of "me", who I was, who I am and who I will be. And this heavy sense of "me and my problems", this is what tortures us.

And yet, as the little bird hops off the tree and flies away, I really cannot seem to find a "me" anywhere.

*

Somewhere deep down, we *all* recognise that we swim in illusions.

You see, I call that thing over there a "bird", but really I have no idea what it is. I call that thing over there a "tree", but really it is a divine mystery that leaves me speechless with bewilderment when I begin to contemplate it. I call that thing over there a "cat", but is that really what it is? The whole damn thing is a mystery, and any explanation I'd give would be simply that, an explanation, an interpretation after the fact, a theory; all mind-stuff overlaid on a reality that is prior to interpretation.

But that thing over there, the thing I point to and call a "cat", is that thing mind-stuff? Is that thing over there, the one I point to and call a "tree", is that mind-stuff? Of course not, you may exclaim, but have you really known anything other than mind-stuff?

Do you really want to know what that thing over there is?

Then let the mind be still. Go, walk over there. Touch that thing we call "tree". Feel its shape, its texture. Listen to it, smell it, even taste it. See the little creatures who call it a home. Look closer; those incredible patterns in the grain of the bark, the moss that grows along its trunk. Look closer, closer. Is it really a "tree"? Does that capture what it is?

You see, it's really nameless, isn't it? It's not a tree at all, is it? It's an experience, an experience that changes with every passing moment, an experience therefore which cannot be named. The word "tree", the concept, the knowledge of it, that is a thing from the past, that is a dead thing. *This*, whatever this is, is alive. It is never the same from one moment to the next.

*

A living thing cannot be captured by a dead thing. Only thought would tell you otherwise.

*

And this "tree" is not really separate from the little creatures that live in it, from the nutrients and micro-organisms in the ground that it feeds on, from the moss that crawls up its side, from the raindrops that it would die without, from the squirrel that has just scrambled up to its tallest branches, from me, as I place my hand on its trunk, as I breathe the air that it too depends on. Everything depends on everything. This 'tree' is not separate from everything else. "Tree" is not separate from the rest of reality, from everything that we call "not tree". Where the hell would I draw the boundary between "tree' and "not Tree"? Where would I slice reality? How would I ever know where to slice? Reality is a unified whole, and thought kills it, cuts it up into little bits, turns it into stale knowledge, processes it in terms of the past, because the mind cannot comprehend the enormity of it all, it cannot begin to fathom the great *mystery* we call life. And so it reduces it, fragments it, calls this a "tree", groups it with all the other things that look similar and calls them all "trees", and does this in the name of knowledge, in the name of science.

But it's a lie, a lie that most of us have been swallowing our entire lives. It's not a tree. It is what it is, and we point to it and call it a tree, and forget that it's not a tree, and that "tree" is mind-stuff, a mental object, an illusion.

But the word "tree" satisfies the mind, doesn't it? Once it has the concept "tree", it can go off and generate all sorts of theories about trees and how they "work". But the trees of knowledge, the trees of science, are trees of the mind. Eat from the tree of the knowledge and you will surely die. You will surely stay locked in the past, a past which tortures you.

But come over here. Feel this bark. Feel it as you contemplate your "tree". Which is real?

Ode to a Particle of Dust

A tiny particle of dust, glittering in a shaft of sun-light, floats lazily down, down, down as I watch from my chair a few feet below. It comes to rest on the bedside table next to its friends: they have scattered over the books and lamp and loose change and cheap plastic alarm clock with its tacky green display.

This very Earth is the Kingdom of Heaven! In this very moment is liberation from all things!

The divine perfection in a particle of dust as it makes its journey from curtain rail to bedside table signifies nothing beyond itself, and everything beyond itself. (The Nothingness behind all form, the Fullness of eve-rything, all this is here!).

And the madness of this world is that we cannot see this perfection, a perfection *inherent* in all things, from the largest to the smallest (and even if we could, it would perhaps just be a temporary distraction, a fleet-ing diversion from the stresses and strains of modern day living...)

But look closer... closer ... and closer still... and the particle of dust reveals its hidden message.

The moment the particle is seen without interpreta-tion, without concept, without an idea of what it is, or has been, or could be, without any preconception as to its function, purpose, or meaning; only when all that madness drops away, the secret is revealed.

The secret? The secret that's as obvious as breathing? It is not a particle of dust at all, but God Himself shining through the emptiness.

So, it all ends here, in this very ordinary room, on this very ordinary day.

Liberation *from* all things; liberation *in* all things; liberation *as* all things.

The sacred in the utterly, utterly, UTTERLY ordinary. And who would have ever guessed?

Doubt

I will doubt everything except doubting. I will doubt everything except this moment, in which there is, unmistakably, doubt arising. I will not, I cannot doubt that. I will doubt the language that is being used to point to the current experience of doubt, I will doubt the verifiability of the experience, but I will not doubt that there is the experience, presently, in this moment. I will doubt that there was experience a moment ago, and I will doubt that there will be experience in a moment's time, but I will not doubt this moment. And though, again, I may doubt everything I can say about existence, and doubt there is "such a thing as existence", I will not and cannot doubt the reality to which the word "existence" points, the reality of this moment, the reality of this, this and this.

So I walk alone in the darkness, the night sky glimmering beyond the warm orange glow of flickering streetlamps, and I doubt it all. *I am, I exist*, that is primary, and all else is nonsense, all else is just mental noise. Before I am something, I am. Before I can know what I am, I am. Before I can doubt that I am, I am. And this undeniable reality of I am-ness is not a mental concept, not a theory to be debated, but a reality to be experienced. And it is fully in your awareness, right now; indeed it is your awareness, right now, so you can never lose it or gain it, it simply *is*, and all you have to do is notice that. When all else has been doubted and discarded, only awareness will be left, only I am-ness.

And then you will literally melt into the divine mystery of this moment, you will simply dissolve in bewilderment at the astonishing fact that you are here at all, that any of this is happening. You will not believe it is possible; you will fall to the ground in amazement at your own existence, at the apparent existence of other things, at the fact there can be apparent relationship between things, between yourself and others; even though in reality there are no others, no things, and certainly no self. You will die, literally die, into the Nothingness of it all, the Nothingness that contains all things, the Nothingness that is total Fullness, the Nothingness/Fullness that is not separate from the apparent things it contains; and you will realise that yes, of course, you *are* that Nothingness/Fullness, you always have been. That Nothingness/Fullness is the essence of it all, the reason for it all, the cause of it all, the beginning and end of it all, for all eternity and beyond....

And you will laugh at even these thoughts, which like all thoughts are just pointless mental noise, and you will simply come to rest in being, in awareness, in the present moment. You will come to deeply accept what life throws at you now, now and now. You will have found your true home, and nothing will ever be able to hurt you again.

The End

And so, we come to the end. And the end is really the beginning.

This is it. We have found Heaven at last. And Heaven was always here, literally right here in front of us. It never left us. And so we didn't really find it at all, because you cannot find something you never lost, can you?

This is Heaven:

Holding this book in your hands.

Breathing. In, out, in, out....

The heart beating in the chest.

The feeling of your bum on the chair.

Thoughts buzzing around in awareness.

Noises in the room.

And all the apparent forms that surround you. Their apparent solidity. Their shape, their colour, their texture. Hardness and softness, lightness and darkness, hot and cold, and all the shades and variations in-between.

See – the miracle is all around, but for some reason we've spent our lives searching for something so much more.

But when this futile search is seen through, by no-one, *this* becomes very interesting indeed. When the search for meaning dissolves, *this* becomes infinitely meaningful, infinitely worthy. When the search for the sacred and divine drops away, God is revealed in all the things of this world.

So take a moment now. Put down this book. Look around you.

This is the only mystery: the fact that you are here, that it is now; that there are things, apparent or otherwise; that there can be movement, time, space; that there appear to be others; that any of this is at all possible...

This is the only miracle, and it's always right in front of us.

And the miracle includes everything. Pain as much as pleasure, hate as much as love. Terrorism, people winning the lottery, heart disease, wars, genocides, daytime television, the whole damn, beautiful mess. Hearts break, tears flow, cancers ravage bodies all over the world – the miracle includes all of that, too.

This is not a book about how "everything is perfect" or how "suffering doesn't exist" or how "there is no self". That would be to reduce the extraordinary complexity and undeniable mystery of life to a simple belief.

Life is, whatever we believe or don't believe. This moment is, however much we resist it, however much we try to escape it. But no escape is really necessary. This world is only a problem from the point of view of a separate individual struggling to make something out of his life before he dies; trying to stay safe, to succeed, to find meaning in a seemingly meaningless world, to be popular, to find love, to avoid pain and suffering...

But as the existence of the separate and isolated individual begins to be seen through, this apparent life story begins to be seen for what it always was: a dream, no more, no less. A narrative playing out in awareness, a story, a movie, a play, a great cosmic game.

A game is only serious when you forget it's a game.

On the surface, then, nothing has changed. There is still emptiness and form, and pain and pleasure, and bodies in motion and at rest, and "me" and "you" and our apparent relationships and complicated life stories, and clouds and trees and rivers and flowers and birds, and babies are still born, and loved ones still die, and the sun still rises and sets, day in, day out....

But underneath it all, there is a love and an equanimity that I will never be able to put into words.

Printed in the United States
85648LV00001B/17/A

9 780955 399909